SUTLIFFIAN
DEEP DIVE DEVOTIONALS

EXODUS:
A JOURNEY OF FAITH

Book 1

Paul Sutliff

Copyright © 2024 Sutliffian Press

All rights reserved.

No part of this book may be reproduced, stored in a retrieval system, or transmitted by any means, electronic, mechanical, photocopying, recording, or otherwise, without written permission from the author.

ISBN (Paperback): 979-8-9921204-3-1
ISBN (eBook): 979-8-9921204-2-4

To the Reader:

It is my sincere wish that this book will help you grow in your faith. Each daily devotion you will find inside was a part of my own daily devotions. I believe that it takes dedication and motivation to serve the one and only King of all creation, the Lord Jesus Christ. In reading this devotional, set aside the same time each day. Include a wake-up prayer before devotions, giving praise to Jesus for another day to give him the glory.

Forward

This book is dedicated to those who are disciples in Christ. It was written for YOU! You are about to embark on a journey of depth in scripture reading. Each day's devotional was part of my personal study. I spent the time to not only read the scripture, but to look at commentaries, to study words and their meanings. I looked at context. Asked questions. Why? Because I believe the Word of God is so important, we have to dig into it to get as much as we can out of it.

What appears a short reading actually takes me about an hour. Prayer, reading His Word, studying the passages, making sure I don't go to fast, have done one important thing to my life. I hold each reading in my heart most of the day. Better yet, each reading serves to arm me for battle, by making scripture not only real, but places the Word in my heart so that I may give answers to those who have questions.

For those struggling with anything some call addictions, which I call binding sin, I believe a daily deep-dive into HIS Word, is the solution. You want out of the sin that binds you to return to it? Grab one of these devotionals. Dig into the Word of God, pray and meditate on what you read. I promise your life will be better. I can say this because my life blossomed as if I had no clue to the wonders of God, before I started this part of my life.

For those scared of doing anything in depth – I am a Special Education Teacher. I write to average people, not scholars. This book was meant for you. It is purposefully written simply for the intent of sharing the deepness and joy of reading God's Word.

If you are a pastor or chaplain doing a prison ministry and are looking for a discount on books. Please contact me at Berean_research@yahoo.com.

DAY #1
EXODUS 1:1-7

1   Now these *are* the names of the children of Israel, which came into Egypt; every man and his household came with Jacob.
2   Reuben, Simeon, Levi, and Judah,
3   Issachar, Zebulun, and Benjamin,
4   Dan, and Naphtali, Gad, and Asher.
5   And all the souls that came out of the loins of Jacob were seventy souls: for Joseph was in Egypt *already*.
6   And Joseph died, and all his brethren, and all that generation.
7   And the children of Israel were fruitful, and increased abundantly, and multiplied, and waxed exceeding mighty; and the land was filled with them.

One of the incredible truths about the Exodus is how many Israelites there were during the time of Joseph. Joseph's family and that of his brothers and their children made up a group of seventy. Today, this amount seems huge, with families having one to two children. But in these times, it was not unusual to have large families. This blossoming family during a time of famine is also a sign of God's blessings. Keep in mind that the only reason the brothers went to Egypt was to get food. God had everything planned out, the reunification of the family, and so much more. They were a band of seventy! Only seventy became as God told Israel, the father of this group, a nation. How mighty is what God blesses? What God is for, no one can stand against! God is one incredible builder!

Dear Lord Jesus,

You, Oh God, are a great planner. You alone arrange what we as men see as impossible. You alone create a chain of causes that create a desired end. Help me to see your hand in planning. Help me to see and grasp even a little of your planning for me. Lord, use me to share your Word with others. That they may see your love and provision.

In Jesus name, Amen.

DAY #2
EXODUS 1:8-14

8   Now there arose up a new king over Egypt, which knew not Joseph.
9   And he said unto his people, Behold, the people of the children of Israel *are* more and mightier than we:
10 Come on, let us deal wisely with them; lest they multiply, and it come to pass, that, when there falls out any war, they join also unto our enemies, and fight against us, and *so* get them up out of the land.
11 Therefore they did set over them taskmasters to afflict them with their burdens. And they built for Pharaoh treasure cities, Pithom and Raamses.
12 But the more they afflicted them, the more they multiplied and grew. And they were grieved because of the children of Israel.

13   And the Egyptians made the children of Israel to serve with rigour:

14   And they made their lives bitter with hard bondage, in mortar, and in brick, and in all manner of service in the field: all their service, wherein they made them serve, *was* with rigour.

We may not think about how honoring God brings us blessings, but this is often the case. We may not even see how much God blesses us. But as usual, others see things differently. They see our being blessed by God as something that seems unfair. They do not believe we deserve whatever blessings we receive. Well, that is where we must agree. We do absolutely nothing to deserve God's goodness, Not one thing.

What we can know is that God keeps his promises. He promises much for simply repenting and calling on his name. Does that mean we all of a sudden receive gifts of gold and cash from heaven? No. What we get is a desire to know more about the God who loved us first. Next, because we want to know more, we start to read the Bible. The book that has been called the "Passport to Life." What is it that sets us apart from others? It is that we desire to please this God who first loved us. We desire to do the things the Bible tells us to do, like "love our neighbor," and "turn the other cheek."

Men of great violence can be turned into men of great peace because of the love of Christ. When people watch and observe, they may even see this change as a great blessing upon the family. They see the change in us as unfair because we suddenly leave what we know for something better, even though it may be totally foreign to us. Just because something in us tells us that following what God wants is better for us than what we want.

Will we be blessed by God for doing these things? YES! Does that mean we will be showered with free money? No. BUT! It does mean that we will not have to worry about where we lay our heads or where our meals will come from. Why? Because we have a growing desire to please God, and that often means doing what is right to provide for our families.

People may get jealous because God honors us with blessings for doing his will. That's ok! They may even get mad seeing how things look good from the outside.

But are we sharing who is blessing us? Are we telling them about this God who loved us first—or are we being silent? Are we being obedient to God in telling others about this great love of God that changed us and made us into who we are? Or, are we more like mice and squeaking by barely if ever mentioning the One whose life and death mean more to us than our own lives?

Dear Lord Jesus,

Thank you for the many blessings you shower on my family and me each day. You continue to plan and prepare things for me. Your love is so endless, I will never grasp how many things you do just to show your love for me. Lord, I ask that you make me a part of those plans and use me to bless others by sharing your great love for me. Use me! Put words in my mouth to tell others of your great love.

In Jesus name, Amen.

DAY #3
EXODUS 1:15-22

15   And the King of Egypt spake to the Hebrew midwives, of which the name of the one *was* Shiphrah, and the name of the other Puah:
16   And he said, When you do the office of a midwife to the Hebrew women, and see *them* upon the stools; if it *be* a son, then ye shall kill him: but if it *be* a daughter, then she shall live.
17   But the midwives feared God, and did not as the King of Egypt commanded them, but saved the men children alive.
18   And the king of Egypt called for the midwives, and said unto them, Why have you done this thing, and have saved the men children alive?
19   And the midwives said unto Pharaoh, Because the Hebrew women *are* not as the Egyptian women; for they *are* lively, and are delivered ere the midwives come in unto them.
20   Therefore God dealt well with the midwives: and the people multiplied, and waxed very mighty.
21   And it came to pass, because the midwives feared God, that he made them houses.
22   And Pharaoh charged all his people, saying, Every son that is born you shall cast into the river, and every daughter you shall save alive.

The Egyptians evolved in their jealousy of Israel being blessed by God. They move to oppression, enslavement, and a desire for bloodshed, which they see as an act too abhorrent to do themselves, an evil and vile sickness called bloodthirstiness. This jealousy intertwined with hatred. Hatred that someone AND NOT THEM is being so blessed. They believe THEY deserve blessings. Not anyone else. This is a sense of superiority, a belief that only Egyptians are fair and goodly people and that they are the best.

In their minds, they are saying these things and looking around, seeing the magnificent masterpieces of architecture perched above those repulsive creatures, their slaves. "Look at all that WE have done, could any other have done such wonders if WE were not blessed? Do we not deserve even more?"

Romans 3:10-18 looks at the heart of man. It sees right into the darkness of the abyss that exists if it is allowed. As it was then in the heart of the leader of the Egyptians.

> As it is written, There is none righteous, no, not one: There is none that understands, there is none that seeks after God. They are all gone out of the way, they are together become unprofitable; there is none that does good, no, not one. Their throat *is* an open sepulchre; with their tongues, they have used deceit; the poison of asps *is* under their lips: Whose mouth *is* full of cursing and bitterness: Their feet *are* swift to shed blood: Destruction and misery *are* in their ways: And the way of peace have they not known: There is no fear of God before their eyes. (Rom 3:10-18 KJV)

A need for control, a sense of superiority over others, and a belief that they alone are above all others (as if they are God) drive Pharaoh into the heart of darkness, prompting him to command such an evil upon the Hebrew people, evil tasks that he could not order his own people to do. —— Until it became irrefutable that his own orders were so shamefully evil and became obviously ignored, He sent his own people to commit the heinous crime that he had first intended to protect them from.

However, the living God is a God of great and awesome power. Nothing is beyond His grasp. He knew all that was happening and had long prepared for such, even the names of the Midwives speak of God's blessings. "Shiphrah" – beauty and "Puah" – Radiance speak to an incredible work that God was about to do.

Dear Lord Jesus,

Lord, may you alone be blessed. May Your name be lifted high in our praises. You know of our troubles long before we experience them. You plan for us. You make the impossible possible. You answer our prayers even before we finish them! Lord, use me as part of Your plans. Allow me to be one of those who share Your boundless love with others. Use me so that I may be the one You choose that will plant the seed by telling others of your work on the cross.

In Jesus' name, Amen.

DAY #4
EXODUS 2:1-4

1\. And there went a man of the house of Levi, and took *to wife* a daughter of Levi.
2\. And the woman conceived, and bare a son: and when she saw him that he *was a* goodly *child*, she hid him three months.
3\. And when she could not longer hide him, she took for him an ark of bulrushes, and daubed it with slime and with

	pitch, and put the child therein; and she laid *it* in the flags by the river's brink.
4	And his sister stood afar off, to wit what would be done to him.

Can you imagine knowing that your child will be killed if you continue to care for him simply because he is a boy? No matter what you do, there is nothing you can do to hide him. He is a healthy and beautiful baby, and there is a law demanding his death. You could kill him yourself, then at least the Egyptian slave masters would not end his life, but your great and loving God is against taking life. You know this in the very core of your being, so you can not do this awful deed. Worse is knowing that even if you simply honor God by keeping the baby boy, you know that should an Egyptian soldier try to kill your child, your husband will fight to the death to protect him. Could you watch this and not fight for the child, knowing you have two more children to care for?

Would you be able to do what Moses' mother does? Would you be able to say God will protect my son? Would you be able to say God will provide? Would you be able to think outside the small confined box of allowed thought to say God has a solution he has already planned out; I just have to believe in it?

Moses' mother does all this. She makes a basket and waterproofs it. This is a step on faith, knowing only that there has to be an alternative. There has to be an act of salvation for her son if she only believes in the loving God who gave her this beautiful boy. Making the basket was easy, it was done with love, and it was a possible solution. She knew she would then not be guilty of killing her child, and she knew then her husband would not find himself compelled to kill to protect them. Those actions compelled each weave, each caress of the basket when applying the waterproofing to be a caress of her love for both God and the child.

Then came the H-U-G-E step… the impossibly big task. It was not only putting the child in the basket, it was putting the basket with the child … into the river. She knew she had to do this, but it hurt so bad she could not even watch should something awful happen. She believed God would create something impossibly good in providing for her son, but she also knew that there were so many possibilities that she could not bear to watch it.

She had her daughter do this. A girl of around 5 years old. Egyptians were not killing girls. She couldn't risk sending Aaron as it'd result in losing both of her sons. Miriam followed the basket in her mother's direction. She had no thoughts of the possible things that could happen. Her daughter had learned who the Creator was. She would even pray with them every day. A child's faith is what we are told is good. It does not question.

Many of us know we probably could not have been as strong as Moses' mother. But are we willing to stand with God today against whatever evil so that others will see that the evil is against t God's Word?

Dear Lord Jesus,

Please continue to mold me and make me into the person You wish. I take great comfort in knowing You are not finished with me yet because I know YOU will make me into something better. Make me into someone who can stand like Moses's mother. Let me be bold and stand up for what is right. Let my words and actions be an example of Your love. Lord, use me so that others may see that what Your word says and promises is much better than anything else they have been told.

In Jesus name, Amen.

DAY #5
EXODUS 2:5-10

5   And the daughter of Pharaoh came down to wash *herself* at the river; and her maidens walked along by the river's side; and when she saw the ark among the flags, she sent her maid to fetch it.
6   And when she had opened *it*, she saw the child: and, behold, the babe wept. And she had compassion on him, and said, *This is* one of the Hebrews' children.
7   Then said his sister to Pharaoh's daughter, Shall I go and call to you a nurse of the Hebrew women, that she may nurse the child for you?
8   And Pharaoh's daughter said to her, Go. And the maid went and called the child's mother.
9   And Pharaoh's daughter said unto her, Take this child away, and nurse it for me, and I will give *you,* your wages. And the woman took the child, and nursed it.
10 And the child grew, and she brought him unto Pharaoh's daughter, and he became her son. And she called his name Moses: and she said, Because I drew him out of the water.

Women understand what happens when a crying infant is around better than any male, and they have just had a baby. Emotions do not influence the start of lactation; It is something biological. The woman may not even notice at first. In general, women are ready for the child to feed upon the cry.

Our God, the great planner – He used this, He knew this was going to happen, and it was the very reason why Miriam, the baby's sister, was sent to watch. For whatever reason, Pharaoh's sister was desirous of having a child. She probably prayed often for the possibility. She must have ached so much for a child that this baby's appearance and cry seemed to fulfill everything she had wished for. The little basket did not make noise. But opening it... the baby cried. Maybe the striking sunlight hit his eyes, waking him. That moment must have been emblazoned on his new adoptive mother's memory forever. Then almost as if impossible, a Hebrew child was present who offered to get her someone to nurse the baby.

The recognition that she could not have given of her own self must have hurt, but the knowledge that someone could and would return the child to her must have also seemed miraculous. Another fulfilled unspoken prayer.

Wet nursing is an occupation women have held throughout history – breastfeeding children who, for whatever reason, were unable to be breastfed by their mothers. Some women lived closely with the wet nurses. Some women sent their babies into the country to be nursed. This occupation, before the existence of formula, seemed to be a highly honorable job. The giving of yourself so that another person's baby might live.

However, breastfeeding alone is not enough to keep a baby alive. A baby needs love. A mother's love, so precious, so wonderful, and in many ways indescribable, is as essential as the milk a baby needs to live. Pharaoh's daughter may never have thanked the little girl who summoned the very mother whose love did not allow her to see her son die and placed him in that very basket he was just drawn from. A woman she would entrust with this newly arrived blessing into the arms of a woman she did not know. The baby was taken into the home of the Hebrew slave until he was weaned.

Imagine being the birth mother of this baby. You could not kill this child and placed your trust in God to protect the child, and

NOW HE WAS RETURNED TO RAISE AND SUCKLE. Such an impossible dream. Even being paid to give what she would have lovingly given her son without a thought. Better still, she could love and raise her son openly, under the protection of those who sought to kill her precious son.

Yes, she knew she would ache when the day came she would have to return him to Pharaoh's daughter. There was no question about that, but she was granted that he would live. This woman of faith must have been singing praises to the God of Abraham every day she held and fed her baby, now named Moses.

Do you have such faith as the mother of Moses? Can you trust in our loving God that he will provide if you just honor what he asks of you?

Dear Lord Jesus,

I praise you for how you protect and provide for me each day. How you do these things is beyond my grasp. Lord, may I trust you and honor you with such faith as the mother of Moses. May my life be one that openly recognizes your incredible love for me and others. Use me Lord to share your great love. Let my mouth not be quiet. Let my mouth express the love You have.

In Jesus name, Amen.

DAY #6
EXODUS 2:11-15

11   And it came to pass in those days, when Moses was grown, that he went out unto his brethren, and looked on their burdens: and he spied an Egyptian smiting a Hebrew, one of his brethren.
12   And he looked this way and that way, and when he saw that *there was* no man, he slew the Egyptian, and hid him in the sand.
13   And when he went out the second day, behold, two men of the Hebrews strove together: and he said to him that did the wrong, Why do you smite your fellow?
14   And he said, Who made you a prince and a judge over us? Do you intend to kill me, as you killed the Egyptian? And Moses feared, and said, "Surely this thing is known!"
15   Now when Pharaoh heard this thing, he sought to slay Moses. But Moses fled from the face of Pharaoh, and dwelt in the land of Midian: and he sat down by a well.

It seems there was a moment when Moses realized who he was, not an Egyptian nephew of the Pharaoh or a Prince of Egypt, but rather the son of slaves. How many times must he have looked out onto them as nothing but lesser humans, like cattle that needed to be shown what to do? But his eyes were opened when he knew that he was also one of these people and not one of the elites of Egypt.

That eye-opening viewpoint, on that day, happened when he saw an Egyptian "smiting" someone who was actually a fellow Hebrew – one of his own people. It's not as if he never saw this before. He was willingly blind. He closed his eyes to all of these before and regarded them as unimportant; he could walk by and not feel a need to be involved. After all, he was one of the elites of Egypt. It wasn't that intervening would be beneath him. It wasn't that seeing Hebrews brutally beaten didn't bother him; it was just that it wasn't important to him at the time. It was "not his place" to interfere. Looking out on "HIS" people, realizing that HE was one of them and nothing he could do could change that, while seeing one of his own savagely beaten, possibly to the edge of death, brought him to the end of being a "bystander."

Moses was so angry watching this that he sought revenge, if not for himself but for his people. He felt angered to such a point that he could no longer act. His mind and body must have raged, calling out for an end to the cruelties done to the Hebrews. He could wait no longer----but he did. He watched and waited … 'til the Egyptian was alone. No one would see him attack. NO ONE would know he was there beating the Egyptian with equal measure. … But the Egyptians died. Moses had killed someone.

He tried to go about his normal life as a "prince." He tried to stand up and do what was normal. But someone saw him kill the man. He was attempting to be fair and kind, but even in that, his act of murder was revealed. His sin found him out. He had to RUN!

Our sins will and do come to the surface. Moses would later write of sin as an action against God versus doing what is right in Numbers 32:23: "But if you will not do so, behold, you have sinned against the LORD: and be sure your sin will find you out."

Dear Lord Jesus,

Lord, my sins are scarlet, they hang like an anchor upon my neck. They are vast, huge, and overwhelming. They will and have uncovered me, laid me naked before others in my shame. Yet how I desire to not have them seen. Lord, I know you have forgiven me for my evils. I know that you have stood in the gap far from my ineptitude. Lord, help me that I should no longer cower in shame but one that stands strong in the changes you have created in me. Let me say that because of God's grace, I am a changed man. May you alone be glorified for the incredible marvels you have worked upon the wheel in molding me into who I am today.

In Jesus name, Amen.

DAY #7
EXODUS 2:16-22

16 Now the priest of Midian had seven daughters: and they came and drew water, and filled the troughs to water their father's flock.
17 And the shepherds came and drove them away: but Moses stood up and helped them, and watered their flock.
18 And when they came to Reuel their father, he said, How *is it that* you have come so soon today?
19 And they said, An Egyptian delivered us out of the hand of the shepherds, and also drew enough water for us, and watered the flock.
20 And he said unto his daughters, "And where *is* he? why *is* it *that* you have left the man? call him, that he may eat bread."
21 And Moses was content to dwell with the man: and he gave Moses Zipporah his daughter.
22 And she bare *him* a son, and he called his name Gershom: for he said, I have been a stranger in a strange land.

Moses was alone. He had been in the desert for a while. Much of that experience was soul-searching talks with the living God that the Hebrews, his brothers, and sisters served. He had left all that he knew to live. He had left behind two families – his Egyptian mother, cousins, and others who were royalty, and his Hebrew biological family, who were slaves and regarded as inferior and of lesser value to the Egyptians.

Moses understood that his crime of murder was not just against the Egyptians but also against the Hebrews, who valued all human life. If all human life has value, surely defenseless people deserve protection. That was likely what was in his mind when he saw the girls attempting to get water for their flocks. He had become a man who could not idly stand by while someone was abused. He had to act; if out of compulsion, so be it because he KNEW it was the right thing to do. A prince of Egypt would not have been wimpy, nor would he have missed opportunities to learn how to fight since he could have been leading armies. He would have been combat-trained as only a royal could be. What would shepherds mean to one such as him? HOW COULD HE NOT ACT?

That one action of protection set another series of events in motion, leading to his no longer being alone. He had pleased the father of his future bride with this one act of kindness. Moses began to understand that   God knew where he was. God knew that he was alone and needed more than a friend to go through life with. Zipporah entered his arms in marriage with blessings from her father, Reul, the priest of Midian.

God blessed the marriage with the gift of a child. Moses must have been living a blissful life, happy and free from the daily conflict that had been in his head about being both a slave and royalty. This was the time for Moses to learn about the God of love. One who loved him so much would not let him be alone.

Dear Lord Jesus,

I thank you that you do not leave me alone. You do not leave me afraid of never being comforted or held. You alone are the great and living God. You know my needs before I know them. Thank you God for being that great provider who gives me more than I desire. Please, Lord, let me be that example of your great love. Use me, Lord, as one who shines a light in the darkness so that others may see You.

In Jesus name, Amen.

DAY #8
EXODUS 2:23-25

23 And it came to pass in process of time, that the King of Egypt died: and the children of Israel sighed by reason of the bondage, and they cried, and their cry came up unto God by reason of the bondage.
24 And God heard their groaning, and God remembered his covenant with Abraham, with Isaac, and with Jacob.
25 And God looked upon the children of Israel, and God had respect unto *them*.

The passage that rings through my head every time I read this is II Chronicles 7:14, "If my people, which are called by my name, shall humble themselves, and pray, and seek my face, and turn from their wicked ways; then will I hear from heaven, and will forgive their sin, and will heal their land." Is that not what happens here?

The Hebrews, who were the blessed of God became fruitful in Egypt to the point of their numbers causing fear amongst the Egyptians, so they enslaved them.

It is so easy to put off worship for the moment, to put off doing devotions, to say wait a minute, I can do that later. Then later becomes an hour – a day, a week – months. It's so easy to put God aside. IT SHOULDN'T BE! When we know we can do better, alarm bells should be going off in our heads!

The Hebrew people may have been blessed by their God, but they forgot to honor Him. Now that they remember Him and think about Him, the world is about to change. God does incredible world-changing things through those he blesses. YES, EVEN YOU!

When you call on God and repent, God uses that. A wild party for your salvation occurs in heaven because you become a part of the family of God.

We can't know what God's plans are or how he intends to use our little footprint on the world to create change. What we can know is that we serve a God who gave His only son so that we may have eternal life! Isn't worshipping him worth the sacrifice of the other things we would put in place of the church, fellowship with other believers, devotions, prayer, and time spent thinking about the things of God?

Dear Lord Jesus,

You love more than I can ever understand. Your love fills me and overwhelms me because that water overflows in abundance. It springs up and dances within me. Lord, let me not forget the wonders you have done in my life. Let me always place you first.

Lord, I beg of you to make me strong! Make me into a strong man of God, unafraid to share your Gospel message! Lord, make my life be that public proclamation that YOU alone are King over me.

In Jesus name, Amen.

DAY #9
EXODUS 3:1-6

1. Now Moses kept the flock of Jethro his father in law, the priest of Midian: and he led the flock to the backside of the desert, and came to the mountain of God, *even* to Horeb.
2. And the angel of the LORD appeared unto him in a flame of fire out of the midst of a bush: and he looked, and, behold, the bush burned with fire, and the bush *was* not consumed.
3. And Moses said, I will now turn aside, and see this great sight, why the bush is not burnt.
4. And when the LORD saw that he turned aside to see, God called unto him out of the midst of the bush, and said, Moses, Moses. And he said, Here *am* I.
5. And he said, Do not come closer: take off your shoes from your feet, for the place whereon you stand *is* holy ground.
6. Moreover he said, I *am* the God of your father, the God of Abraham, the God of Isaac, and the God of Jacob. And Moses hid his face; for he was afraid to look upon God.

Moses was going about his business caring for the flocks of sheep. He was no longer a proud Egyptian royal but a lowly shepherd. He did his job to the best of his ability. Part of doing this meant scanning the area around his flock for dangers. Moses was working. He was not out for a stroll. He was on the job when he saw what looked like a bush that was blazing with fire…but somehow … somehow, the fire was not going out, and … the bush was not being consumed.

Humans are curious when we see things that seem to be playing tricks on our eyes. We do a quick double-take, blink, take another look, then want to get closer to see if what we see is actually what we think we are seeing. Moses was no different than most of us. He got closer.

When Moses got closer, God called out to him. In the Cecil B. DeMille movie, God has this booming voice. Its sound resonates (echoes within you). This voice knew his name. It was a personal call to him. It was not "Hey you, shepherd man. Yes, you." This is a personal call from a God who knows his name, a God who, in all his magnificence and glory, calls man by his name.

Hearing his name called, Moses does not cower in fear but seeks to come even closer. Where is this voice coming from? Who is it that calls his name? How does it know who he is?

God seems to know all that Moses is thinking. He answers, "Do not come closer: take off your shoes from your feet, for the place whereon you stand *is* holy ground" (vs. 5). How does one respond to this but with quick, immediate action, ripping the shoes off your feet, bowing or laying in total submission to this holy one.

Today, God stands and knocks on the door of your heart, calling you by name. He knows you more than you know yourself. He hears your inward cries of frustration and desires. He knows you more than anyone else. Can you say no to God?

This is one of the unexplained strange things. God gave us the ability to say no to Him. We are not robots. We are able to make our own choices. That does not mean we always make the right ones.

What happens if you answer God with a "here I am"? Are you ready to kneel before the one whose royalty outshines the brightest star? Is that what God asks? No, God simply told him to take off his shoes. Did Moses kneel or bow? Probably. Moses hid his face. Being in the presence of holiness and being a man stained with sin is a humbling experience.

Moses' response led to God introducing himself. In many ways, this introduction is not a lecture. It is just part of a conversation. Moses' God is a personal God! Everything Moses hears from God is about who he is and his proven authority. When men introduce themselves to other men, they share what they do and often who they work for. Why? Men like to know who a person is and if the person they are meeting has any authority or use over them. Imagine this introduction being given by God to you.

God is standing at the door of your heart and knocking. Answer that door. Have that conversation with the living God.

Dear Lord Jesus,

You know me more than I know myself. Yet you love me knowing I have chosen to do so many wrongs, even things I think were evil. How you can have such love is beyond my own comprehension. Lord, use me. Use me so that I may share your love reaching beyond barriers, reaching to those who think themselves incapable of being loved. Lord, I know you are the God of Love. Use me.

In Jesus name, Amen.

DAY #10
EXODUS 3:7-15

7   And the LORD said, I have surely seen the affliction of my people which *are* in Egypt, and have heard their cry by reason of their taskmasters; for I know their sorrows;

8   And I am come down to deliver them out of the hand of the Egyptians, and to bring them up out of that land unto a good land and a large, unto a land flowing with milk and honey; unto the place of the Canaanites, and the Hittites, and the Amorites, and the Perizzites, and the Hivites, and the Jebusites.

9   Now therefore, behold, the cry of the children of Israel is come unto me: and I have also seen the oppression wherewith the Egyptians oppress them.

10   Come now therefore, and I will send you unto Pharaoh, that you may bring forth my people the children of Israel out of Egypt.

11   And Moses said unto God, Who *am* I, that I should go unto Pharaoh, and that I should bring forth the children of Israel out of Egypt?

12   And he said, Certainly I will be with you; and this *shall be* a token unto you, that I have sent you: When you have brought forth the people out of Egypt, you shall serve God upon this mountain.

13   And Moses said unto God, Behold, when I come unto the children of Israel, and shall say unto them, The God of your fathers hath sent me unto you; and they shall say to me, What *is* his name? what shall I say unto them?

14 And God said unto Moses, I AM THAT I AM: and he said, Thus shalt you say unto the children of Israel, I AM hath sent me unto you.

15 And God said moreover unto Moses, Thus shalt you say unto the children of Israel, The LORD God of your fathers, the God of Abraham, the God of Isaac, and the God of Jacob, hath sent me unto you: this *is* my name for ever, and this *is* my memorial unto all generations.

When Moses' adoptive Uncle, the Pharaoh died, there was great sadness in Egypt. The Hebrew people, the Chosen of God, took this time to pray to God. They turned and called on His name. They repented and begged for His mercy, His deliverance. This is in the last few verses of chapter 2.

God is now having a conversation with Moses and tells him that HE, the living and all-powerful God, has heard the cry of His people, and HE will deliver them. For Moses, this could have been enough to make him joyous. After all, they were his people. But why was the living God sharing this with him, a former prince now a shepherd?

In verse 8, God is very specific, telling Moses of a place He will bring His people. HE speaks of something that seems almost dream-like, "a land flowing with milk and honey." For many of us who are not farmers, we hear this, and it seems fantastical. But to the farmer hearing this passage, his ears perked up. What he hears are two words: "fertile soil."

In verse 10, Moses learns why God shares these exciting things with him. Moses is part of God's plan. God plans to use Moses to help deliver His people.

Imagine being told by God that he plans to use you. Would you dare to respond, "BUT WHO AM I?" God is loving, and even this questioning of Moses is taken and accepted. Man can not understand his part in God's plan. Moses has a chance to be used by the great and living God and questions his own ability, not God's.

God continues the conversation with Moses telling him that HE, the very real God, will be with him. So, it is not who Moses is. This is all about who God is. Suddenly, the fear of being killed for having committed an act of murder in Egypt seems small. Even though he knew this was possible if he returned to Egypt, he was to "go with God." God tells Moses of a plan for where the people will go first after leaving Pharaoh's control. To the very mountain, they are now having this conversation. This event, so seemingly impossible, will have a complete circle. He will go and return with God's people to this very spot.

Suddenly Moses realizes how little he knows his own people, the Hebrews. He does not even know the name of their God. Surely, if God is who they prayed to, they know his name and will expect him to know also. Right?

God gives his name, "I AM WHO I AM." It is not the name of any Egyptian god or goddess Moses has ever known. It is the name of God so superior and vast when compared to their tiny selves. God tells Moses the genealogy of faith that he would be expected to know if he is one of the Hebrews.

God shared his plans with Moses, included him in the plans, and now Moses was soon to be sent to a land that had promised to execute him. This is why prayers to the living God should not be all one-sided with our pleadings and praises. We must also listen to know how we fit in God's plans.

Dear Lord Jesus,

You alone are the Great "I AM." You alone set the moon and the stars in their places. Yet your loving kindness includes me in your plans. You have died so I may have eternal life. How may I serve you, Lord? What are your plans for me? Talk to me about your plans and how you will use me. Lord, help me to listen to you also. Help me to hear your call.

In Jesus name, Amen.

DAY #11
EXODUS 3:15-22

15   And God said moreover unto Moses, Thus shall you say unto the children of Israel, The LORD God of your fathers, the God of Abraham, the God of Isaac, and the God of Jacob, has sent me unto you: this *is* my name for ever, and this *is* my memorial unto all generations.

16   Go, and gather the elders of Israel together, and say unto them, The LORD God of your fathers, the God of Abraham, of Isaac, and of Jacob, appeared unto me, saying, I have surely visited you, and seen that which is done to you in Egypt:

17   And I have said, I will bring you up out of the affliction of Egypt unto the land of the Canaanites, and the Hittites, and the Amorites, and the Perizzites, and the Hivites, and the Jebusites, unto a land flowing with milk and honey.

18   And they shall listen to your voice: and you shall come, you and the elders of Israel, unto the King of Egypt, and

you shall say unto him, The LORD God of the Hebrews has met with us: and now let us go, we beseech you, three days' journey into the wilderness, that we may sacrifice to the LORD our God.

19   And I am sure that the King of Egypt will not let you go, no, not by a mighty hand.

20   And I will stretch out my hand, and smite Egypt with all my wonders which I will do in the midst thereof: and after that he will let you go.

21   And I will give this people favour in the sight of the Egyptians: and it shall come to pass, that, when you go, you shall not go empty.

22   But every woman shall borrow of her neighbour, and of her that sojourns in her house, jewels of silver, and jewels of gold, and raiment: and you shall put *them* upon your sons, and upon your daughters; and you shall spoil the Egyptians.

Some of the word choices of God here slightly reveal who He is versus who we are. "And I am sure that…" is something we say when we feel something is likely to happen. When God is sure, it's a done deal.

God tells Moses to tell his people that this will not be an easy thing. The deliverance he promises will not happen quickly with a magical hand wiping away the bondage of Israel. He does promise "to smite Egypt with all HIS wonders."

What would you think if Moses came to you, the Hebrew slave, and said this? Would you be wondering how many are all? Would you groan and complain that enough is enough, just let us go? Would you question how God could use a Hebrew prince of Egypt? Even saying that during this time probably left a bad taste in their mouth, thinking of a betrayer. But would he exist without God's hand preserving him?

Better still, would you laugh at the picture in your mind of the Egyptians covering your women in their best clothing and jewels knowing it may never be seen again? The picture given here is not just one of punishment but an unbelievable, unimaginable one.

YET THAT IS A PICTURE OF VICTORY! A victorious triumph. Think about it this way, The Egyptian gods claimed victory in enslaving the people of the Hebrew God. But then, after having enslaved the Hebrews for a time, their people gave their best jewelry and best clothes to those they enslaved, begging them to go. What does it say about the superiority of GOD over the incredible smallness of the Egyptian gods?

God promises victory. That is His message. It is not just one of freedom and deliverance but one of victory. Think about what Christ has done for you and me. Is that not the same? Is Christ's work of His shed blood for us, not a Victory and far more than freedom and deliverance?

There is an old hymn called "The Victory of Jesus" that tells so much about this Victory.

```
Victory in Jesus                          from www.traditionalmusic.co.uk
1.
I heard an old, old story, How a Savior came from glory,
How He gave His life on Calvary To save a wretch like me;
I heard about His groaning, Of His precious blood's atoning,
Then I repented of my sins And won the victory.

Cho.
O victory in Jesus, My Savior, forever,
He sought me and bought me With His redeeming blood;
He loved me ere I knew Him And all my love is due Him,
He plunged me to victory, Beneath the cleansing flood.

2.
I heard about His healing, Of His cleansing pow'r revealing,
How He made the lame to walk again And caused the blind to see;
And then I cried "Dear Jesus, Come and heal my broken spirit,"
And somehow Jesus came and bro't To me the victory.
3.
I heard about a mansion He has built for me in glory,
And I heard about the streets of gold Beyond the crystal sea;
About the angels singing, And the old, redemption story,
And some sweet day I'll sing up there The song of victory.
```

Dear Lord Jesus,

Work on me Lord, let me be one who clearly hears Your Word. Let me be one who acts to do that which is right. Lord, You are the GOD OF VICTORY! You alone grant us such a prize of victory it's hard for us to comprehend it even until the moment we die. Lord, let me share this incredible victory that YOU have won for us. Let me be the one who gets the chance to share this great love You have for us.

In Jesus name, Amen.

DAY #12
EXODUS 4:1-9

1   And Moses answered and said, But, behold, they will not believe me, nor hearken unto my voice: for they will say, The LORD hath not appeared unto you.
2   And the LORD said unto him, What *is* that in your hand? And he said, A rod.
3   And he said, Cast it on the ground. And he cast it on the ground, and it became a serpent; and Moses fled from before it.
4   And the LORD said unto Moses, Put forth your hand, and take it by the tail. And he put forth his hand, and caught it, and it became a rod in his hand:

5	That they may believe that the LORD God of their fathers, the God of Abraham, the God of Isaac, and the God of Jacob, hath appeared unto you.
6	And the LORD said furthermore unto him, Put now your hand into your bosom. And he put his hand into his bosom: and when he took it out, behold, his hand *was* leprous as snow.
7	And he said, Put your hand into your bosom again. And he put his hand into his bosom again; and plucked it out of his bosom, and, behold, it was turned again as his *other* flesh.
8	And it shall come to pass, if they will not believe you, neither hearken to the voice of the first sign, that they will believe the voice of the latter sign.
9	And it shall come to pass, if they will not believe also these two signs, neither hearken unto your voice, that you shall take of the water of the river, and pour *it* upon the dry *land*: and the water which you take out of the river shall become blood upon the dry *land*.

Moses has heard God's call. His response starts with, "BUT they will not believe me." You almost feel like screaming NO – WRONG ANSWER! Yet we serve a personal God. One who does not seem to mind our talking with Him, even when we disagree. It is OK that we are wrong, sometimes, we just need more from God to stand taller. This is still a conversation. It takes two to have a conversation. Think of how well-prepared Moses was because of this being a conversation. When you serve a God who is able to know your answer before you even respond, you get a well-prepared answer. "But what if they do not believe me...." Who is "they" here? The Hebrews in captivity, or is he talking about the Egyptians or both? Moses is speaking primarily of his own people who barely know him. As much as it sounds bad to have said this, you have to ask yourself would you believe a stranger or someone you know more. God gave him signs to prove who sent him. These signs were to convince the Hebrew people that the great I AM indeed had sent Moses. God was demonstrative, He had Moses see each one of those signs. This must have given him a level of confidence. God did not give him one sign. NO, he gave Moses five signs! 1) rod to snake 2) snake to rod 3) normal to leprous hand 4) leprous to normal hand, and 5) Water to blood. FIVE SIGNS! It's almost as if God is saying, "yes, my people are stubborn and do not listen to just anyone."

Would you have listened to someone you barely know after he returned and claimed to be sent by God? I think I might have needed some convincing. Would this make his message more powerful when it is delivered? INDEED! God's answer here makes the message He is asking Moses to deliver one of great power.

Dear Lord Jesus,

You love even me. It baffles me how that is possible despite everything I've done. You even make special plans just for me. You prepare the way in which I will go. Lord, you embolden me and use me so that I may share Your word with others.

In Jesus name, Amen.

DAY #13
EXODYS 4:10-18

10   And Moses said unto the LORD, O my Lord, I *am* not eloquent, neither heretofore, nor since you have spoken unto your servant: but I *am* slow of speech, and of a slow tongue.
11   And the LORD said unto him, Who hath made man's mouth? or who makes the dumb, or deaf, or the seeing, or the blind? have not I the LORD?
12   Now therefore go, and I will be with your mouth, and teach you what you shall say.
13   And he said, O my Lord, send, I pray you, by the hand *of him whom* you will send.
14   And the anger of the LORD was kindled against Moses, and he said, *is* not Aaron the Levite your brother? I know that he can speak well. And also, behold, he comes forth to meet you: and when he sees you, he will be glad in his heart.
15   And you shalt speak unto him, and put words in his mouth: and I will be with your mouth, and with his mouth, and will teach you what you shall do.
16   And he shall be your spokesman unto the people: and he shall be, *even* he shall be to you instead of a mouth, and you shalt be to him instead of God.
17   And you shalt take this rod in your hand, wherewith you shalt do signs.
18   And Moses went and returned to Jethro his father in law, and said unto him, Let me go, I pray you, and return unto my brethren which *are* in Egypt, and see whether they be yet alive. And Jethro said to Moses, Go in peace.

Moses' conversation with God changes when Moses seems to forget who he is talking with. Perhaps, having spent so much time around polytheists, his own concept of God was so limited that he had difficulty realizing that the God of the Hebrews was, is, and will be all-powerful. It is one thing to recognize how unworthy you are of what God has for you to do. It is quite another to come up with a string of excuses. After all, when you are talking to the God who created the universe, the very God who gave you existence and a voice, it would be better to recognize that all things are possible with God. When he called Moses, do you think that God did not know Moses was ashamed of how poorly he spoke? Did Moses think God did not know he stuttered?

God knew who Moses was when He CALLED HIM BY NAME! Our God is a God of the Impossible. He does impossible things. He makes what seems impossible tangible and better—So real that no one can deny it.

Moses seems still unsure of this God of wonder who had just sent him off when he approaches his father-in-law. He awkwardly asks to let him go back to Egypt. It seems he does not tell Jethro why he would want to go back. The truth is Moses probably did not want to go back. But God told him to be HIS voice to his people and to speak to the Egyptians.

Maybe Moses still did not grasp how God had planned so much for him. Even before God called Moses by name, he had allowed someone to tell Moses' brethren that he was alive and living in Midian. That his brother Aaron, a slave with no permission to go, had found a way to leave to seek him out. This great God knows us better than we know ourselves. God planned for Moses, knowing how he would react and what his answers would be.

Can you see how much this great big God loves even you? Stop and look at the things that happen today. Could they have happened if God did not make them possible? This is a slight look at how much God loves you and makes things happen just for you! How great is HIS love for even us

Dear Lord Jesus,

    We are lowly sinners. We do not deserve a thimble full of love from you. We desire things that are not of you. We want things that you would have us say no to. How is it that your love is so great and is even for me? How can you love me? Lord, you chose Moses. You called him by name. You even allowed him to have his brother help. Lord, call my name. Lord, send me. Use me that I should share of your greatness, your great and undying love shown in your shed blood for us. Please, Lord—use me.

In Jesus name, Amen.

DAY #14
EXODUS 4:19-23

19   And the LORD said unto Moses in Midian, Go, return into Egypt: for all the men are dead which sought your life.

20   And Moses took his wife and his sons, and set them upon an ass, and he returned to the land of Egypt: and Moses took the rod of God in his hand.

21   And the LORD said unto Moses, When you go to return into Egypt, see that you do all those wonders before Pharaoh, which I have put in your hand: but I will harden his heart, that he shall not let the people go.

22   And you shall say unto Pharaoh, Thus saith the LORD, Israel *is* my son, *even* my firstborn:
23   And I say unto you, Let my son go, that he may serve me: and if you refuse to let him go, behold, I will slay your son, *even* your firstborn.

The order of how things happen here seems a little muddled in the way we think today. Many of us would have told our wives first. Then asked our father-in-law's permission if we needed it. Moses was, in some ways, like Jonah, it seems, and not eager to be God's chosen vessel. So He tells Moses to get moving again. Maybe he knew how much she loved her father and sisters and may not have wanted to leave them. For whatever reason, it seems Moses was not eager to push on. He needed to hear God once more.

Moses does as he is told, puts his wife and child on a donkey, and prepares to go. Moses is no longer poor. Note that he does not bring his herd with him. Nothing is said of him, and his wife preparing to leave. Think about this. Would it be considered smart to bring your wealth with you to a place you will be considered a slave? Moses knew what he was now leaving behind and going back to. There is nothing here telling us that Zipporah knew beyond anything her husband had shared with her.

Moses is reminded to do as God asked of him. He is told the answer will be "no." Do you like being told no?

Pay special attention to these last few verses. God tells Moses to say that Israel is His son, even his firstborn. The literary term for this could be foreshadowing, speaking of something to come. But I believe this is different. It is not foreshadowing but God preparing Pharaoh for his last choice of words that lead to the last plague.

We know that God works on us to get us to where we are. Every little thing that makes us who we are is, in every sense molding and shaping us into who we will become. Is this not what God does for us to make us better and stronger believers in Him?

Dear Lord Jesus,

I give you the glory for being the only one worthy of my worship. You alone can stop a hurricane, squash a tornado, end a blinding snowstorm, calm an earthquake, and so much more. Lord, you chose me! Let me serve you and glorify your name! Let me be the one to say YES, HE IS MY GOD! Let me be the one to share your great love and wonders. Lord, please use me. Do not let me be quiet. Do not let me say no, I can't do that. Make my faith in you stronger and bolder. That I would be one who can claim my love for You grows each day!

In Jesus name, Amen.

DAY #15
EXODUS 4:24-26

24   And it came to pass by the way in the inn, that the LORD met him, and sought to kill him.
25   Then Zipporah took a sharp stone, and cut off the foreskin of her son, and cast *it* at his feet, and said, Surely a bloody husband *are* you to me.
26   So he let him go: then she said, A bloody husband *you are*, because of the circumcision.

The law had not yet been given. But circumcision had been a gift for men's outward expression of faith. It was something done for Moses and something he should have known that set him apart from his Egyptian friends. But it is unlikely that his mother knowing this would have allowed him to be in a locker room-type situation. Traditionally, circumcision is done on the 8th day after birth. The action of circumcision gets to be very painful if you are older. Moses's son rode the ass along with his mother. This means he was at least the age of a toddler.

God met them. He confronted them about not being fully committed or not believing as they should because this – circumcision still had to be done.

Zipporah, not Moses, does this deed. Perhaps the confrontation was for her to hear God. Maybe it was so she could understand that God was indeed alive and her husband was part of His plans. God needed her to be a woman of faith for her husband. This push by God made the plan HE had for them work.

Dear Lord Jesus,

Women are so precious in your sight. You work through them too. You bless marriages by making them companions. You, the great planner, see goodness in not having a man be alone. You, Lord, made Zipporah a partner with Moses in his return to the land that had enslaved his people. This very real action of circumcision made her one with the Hebrew people. This had been the only thing separating them. Lord, your plans always bear fruit – Good fruit. Lord, let me not forget that there is indeed greatness in sharing Your word with those who do not know you. Your plans—your work is always far better. Help me to trust in you.

In Jesus name, Amen.

DAY #16
EXODUS 4:27-31

27   And the LORD said to Aaron, Go into the wilderness to meet Moses. And he went, and met him in the mount of God, and kissed him.
28   And Moses told Aaron all the words of the LORD who had sent him, and all the signs which he had commanded him.
29   And Moses and Aaron went and gathered together all the elders of the children of Israel:
30   And Aaron said all the words which the LORD had spoken unto Moses, and did the signs in the sight of the people.
31   And the people believed: and when they heard that the LORD had visited the children of Israel and that he had looked upon their affliction, then they bowed their heads and worshipped.

When God sends a message of hope to His people, he gives a clear introduction. Remember, Aaron had already set out while Moses was on the mountain. Moses does not even leave the mountain, and Aaron is there! This shows the likely timing of his arrival when Moses comes down from having seen the burning bush. It is possible that there were more conversations between God and Moses, but this is more likely.

This brief piece may have Moses, including his brother, who he had not known most of his life. Including Aaron may have been incredibly important at the beginning. Can you imagine the difficulties that would have existed had God not already sent him?

He was in some ways, like John the Baptist, preparing a way for Christ. Moses knew of Aaron's speaking ability. This is also likely because Aaron had served in a leadership role. It is also possible that Moses observed the people's response to him at some point before he had to leave Egypt. This means that movies depicting Aaron as meek and servile are wrong.

Aaron is sent as a helper to Moses. He serves in that role only. He is not God's second choice.

It is interesting to note that Aaron and Moses present to the elders of the children of Israel. This means that they had some form of organization that existed. The elders needed the signs and wonders to be convinced that God had sent Moses. The elders believe and then share that message of hope with the people of Israel. Every step of the way, God is in the process.

Dear Lord Jesus,

Help me to have faith where things seem impossible. Help me to be willing and able to stand and be your representative of what is right when the world seems so stuck in error. Lord Jesus, strengthen and embolden me so I may share your word with others. Let me see the power of your Gospel. Let me be the one to plant seeds. I want to be a part of your plan today; even though I know I am, sometimes I just want to see it. Lord, work on me. Make me into that one who, like Moses, stands unafraid, knowing You are on my side.

In Jesus name, Amen.

DAY #17
EXODUS 5:1-21

1 And afterward Moses and Aaron went in, and told Pharaoh, Thus saith the LORD God of Israel, Let my people go, that they may hold a feast unto me in the wilderness.

2 And Pharaoh said, Who *is* the LORD, that I should obey his voice to let Israel go? I know not the LORD, neither will I let Israel go.

3 And they said, The God of the Hebrews has met with us: let us go, we pray you, three days' journey into the desert, and sacrifice unto the LORD our God; lest he fall upon us with pestilence, or with the sword.

4 And the King of Egypt said unto them, Wherefore do you, Moses and Aaron, let the people from their works? get you unto your burdens.

5 And Pharaoh said, Behold, the people of the land now *are* many, and you make them rest from their burdens.

6 And Pharaoh commanded the same day the taskmasters of the people, and their officers, saying,

7 You shall no more give the people straw to make brick, as heretofore: let them go and gather straw for themselves.

8 And the tale of the bricks, which they did make heretofore, you shall lay upon them; you shall not diminish *ought* thereof: for they *be* idle; therefore they cry, saying, Let us go *and* sacrifice to our God.

9 Let there more work be laid upon the men, that they may labour therein; and let them not regard vain words.

10 And the taskmasters of the people went out, and their officers, and they spoke to the people, saying, Thus saith Pharaoh, I will not give you straw.

11 Go you, get you straw where you can find it: yet not ought of your work shall be diminished.

12 So the people were scattered abroad throughout all the land of Egypt to gather stubble instead of straw.

13 And the taskmasters hasted *them*, saying, Fulfil your works, *your* daily tasks, as when there was straw.

14 And the officers of the children of Israel, which Pharaoh's taskmasters had set over them, were beaten, *and* demanded, Why have you not fulfilled your task in making brick both yesterday and to day, as before?

15 Then the officers of the children of Israel came and cried unto Pharaoh, saying, Why do you deal thus with your servants?

16 There is no straw given unto your servants, and they say to us, Make brick: and, behold, your servants *are* beaten; but the fault *is* in your own people.

17 But he said, You *are* idle, *you are* idle: therefore you say, Let us go *and* do sacrifice to the LORD.

18 Go therefore now, *and* work; for there shall no straw be given you, yet shall you deliver the tale of bricks.

19 And the officers of the children of Israel did see *that* they *were* in evil case, after it was said, You shall not diminish *ought* from your bricks of your daily task.

20 And they met Moses and Aaron, who stood in the way, as they came forth from Pharaoh:

21 And they said unto them, The LORD look upon you, and judge; because you have made our savour to be abhorred in the eyes of Pharaoh, and in the eyes of his servants, to put a sword in their hand to slay us.

The first thing noticed here is that Moses and Aaron were somehow responsible for the people not working. The people, in general, stopped working because they hoped to be freed shortly or they were directed to stop working.

Pharaoh's punishment of the Hebrew people is to remove the straw from the brick-making process. This is in truth, sheer stupidity as it removes the strength of the brick. The bricks might bake and appear equal in strength, but they are much more susceptible to the environment and will fall apart with a little pressure.

Moses and Aaron spoke to Pharaoh this time, not with the words of the Lord alone. They added some things, saying God threatened them. They also seemed unprepared for how quickly they were shut down and shown the door. Moses and Aaron knew Pharaoh was going to tell them no this time. They were cut off so abruptly that no wonders were shown on this first encounter.

The elders of Israel had been told that Pharaoh would not say yes the first time. You have to wonder if they told their people this part of the message that God was going to deliver them. The people come to Moses and Aaron full of anger. Saying things like, "it's all your fault."

Dear Lord Jesus,

Help me to face life prepared to share your Word. Please do not let me add or take away from your Word. Lord, work on me. Help me to plan out what to say when people say no.

In Jesus name, Amen.

DAY #18
EXODUS 5:22-6:1

22   And Moses returned unto the LORD, and said, Lord, wherefore have you *so* evil entreated this people? why *is* it *that* you have sent me?
23   For since I came to Pharaoh to speak in your name, he has done evil to this people; neither have you delivered your people at all.
6:1 Then the LORD said unto Moses, Now shall you see what I will do to Pharaoh: for with a strong hand shall he let them go, and with a strong hand shall he drive them out of his land.

We often complain that we are a society that wants things "RIGHT NOW!" We nuke our food. OKAY, microwave it. We carry cell phones so we can get our messages, emails, and phone calls right now. We hate standing in lines. Stores have people called front-end managers assigned to deal with that issue. We don't want to wait. We want everything NOW! From what we eat to the moment we go to sleep, we want it Now.

You would think of anyone we should get it. We should understand what happened here. God told them beforehand that Pharaoh would not let HIS people go. Moses and Aaron told the elders all that God had told them. Did the elders tell them this would be swift, or did they simply say we are to be delivered from the Egyptian taskmasters? Would they have reacted differently if they had heard about God's promise to deliver them but not immediately?

Consider how selfishly we want things right now! Possibly the answer is NO!

Moses himself, who heard it straight from God seems to have forgotten in his plea to God. He questions what happened, why was it not immediately? And why did Pharaoh not listen? Moses had been told it would not happen quickly. If Moses had difficulty grasping this, consider how hard it would be for an average person.

"But God is good and means it for the best" is an old Jewish statement that truly fits here. God meant this refusal of Pharaoh to serve HIS desires. God told Moses, "NOW shall you see what I will do to Pharaoh." That NOW is what Moses and the Israelites so wanted and needed. We serve a God so big He knows our desires before we know them. The people needed to see God standing up for them. NOW they are going to see that.

Dear Lord Jesus!

Help me in my desire to seek your timing, not my own. I'm not asking for patience; I'm asking for assistance in understanding and waiting on your schedule as best I can. This is a concept so big it's hard for me to grasp. Lord, I don't need things right now as much as I want them answered and granted right now. I want them at your perfect time. Help me to see how you plan for me in this. Lord, allow my desire to seek your will for my life to become an example to others. Let others see the joy I have in serving you. For it is in You alone that this joy is possible.

In Jesus name, Amen.

DAY #19
EXODUS 6:2-9

2   And God spoke unto Moses, and said unto him, I *am* the LORD:
3   And I appeared unto Abraham, unto Isaac, and unto Jacob, by *the name of* God Almighty, but by my name JEHOVAH was I not known to them.
4   And I have also established my covenant with them, to give them the land of Canaan, the land of their pilgrimage, wherein they were strangers.
5   And I have also heard the groaning of the children of Israel, whom the Egyptians keep in bondage; and I have remembered my covenant.
6   Wherefore say unto the children of Israel, I *am* the LORD, and I will bring you out from under the burdens of the Egyptians, and I will rid you out of their bondage, and I will redeem you with a stretched out arm, and with great judgments:
7   And I will take you to me for a people, and I will be to you a God: and you shall know that I *am* the LORD your God, which bringeth you out from under the burdens of the Egyptians.
8   And I will bring you in unto the land, concerning the which I did swear to give it to Abraham, to Isaac, and to Jacob; and I will give it you for an heritage: I *am* the LORD.
9   And Moses spoke so unto the children of Israel: but they hearkened not unto Moses for anguish of spirit, and for cruel bondage.

This is the second conversation that Moses had with God. A conversation where God reminds him just who HE is. God tells Moses that HE keeps his promises. God tells Moses that HE is bigger than time. He is the only one who his forefathers Abraham, Issac, and Jacob served. Yet, Moses has been granted something special – the chance to know the name of God! Is that not something personal?

God reminds Moses once more that His action would be powerful and would take time. God speaks of HIS GREAT judgments. PLURAL. God is going to do something very publicly that no one can deny. Not one of the children of Israel will be able to deny it is the Lord who has saved them from a life of slavery. Not one! This response of the living God is filled with promises. It is filled with the foresight of what is to come.

But we are so selfish and want things now. Humans are also scared of change. To think that their God would listen to their pleas and then reject them when God revealed HIS plan? It's so hard to accept, but people seem to like living in fear. They would rather believe the horror of living as a slave than of the freedom offered and promised by the living God whom their ancestors served.

Slaves do not have to sacrifice their beliefs. They may be beaten into submitting physically to the desires of their slave masters. But that does not mean they must sacrifice who they are as humans. Sacrificing hope in the name of fear is a horrible and unfathomable choice. Can you imagine giving up hope?

As Christians, our hope is in Christ Jesus, our Lord. He paid the price for our sins. He has done more than we can even imagine. We have access to the living God as individuals, thanks to this wonder-working power of the one who first loved us. We can each seek out the One of our hope through prayer. Can you conceive of giving up your personal freedoms and then adding hope that is in Christ on that altar of sacrifice as part of your enslavement?

I for one say NO to slavery. Though others may place chains on me, my hope which is in Christ Jesus shall never leave me. Can we allow fear to enslave us? Fear that envelopes us and eats away at our boldness in Jesus? NO! We must LIVE for Christ.

Dear Lord Jesus,

You are the great and living God who gave all that I may have life. Your sacrifice is what gives me hope. Your love is beyond my understanding. How can I return any less than boldness and love of You? What you desire is the salvation of so many to be joint heirs with You. Your love WAS and IS a bold expression. Lord, take away my shyness that I may share of this great love you have. Let me share my Hope which is in You!

In Jesus name, Amen.

DAY #20
EXODUS 6:10-32

10   And the LORD spoke unto Moses, saying,
11   Go in, speak unto Pharaoh king of Egypt, that he let the children of Israel go out of his land.
12   And Moses spoke before the LORD, saying, Behold, the children of Israel have not hearkened unto me; how then shall Pharaoh hear me, who *am* of uncircumcised lips?

13 And the LORD spoke unto Moses and unto Aaron, and gave them a charge unto the children of Israel, and unto Pharaoh king of Egypt, to bring the children of Israel out of the land of Egypt.

14 These *be* the heads of their fathers' houses: The sons of Reuben the firstborn of Israel; Hanoch, and Pallu, Hezron, and Carmi: these *be* the families of Reuben.

15 And the sons of Simeon; Jemuel, and Jamin, and Ohad, and Jachin, and Zohar, and Shaul the son of a Canaanitish woman: these *are* the families of Simeon.

16 And these *are* the names of the sons of Levi according to their generations; Gershon, and Kohath, and Merari: and the years of the life of Levi *were* an hundred thirty and seven years.

17 The sons of Gershon; Libni, and Shimi, according to their families.

18 And the sons of Kohath; Amram, and Izhar, and Hebron, and Uzziel: and the years of the life of Kohath *were* an hundred thirty and three years.

19 And the sons of Merari; Mahali and Mushi: these *are* the families of Levi according to their generations.

20 And Amram took him Jochebed his father's sister to wife; and she bare him Aaron and Moses: and the years of the life of Amram *were* an hundred and thirty and seven years.

21 And the sons of Izhar; Korah, and Nepheg, and Zichri.

22 And the sons of Uzziel; Mishael, and Elzaphan, and Zithri.

23 And Aaron took him Elisheba, daughter of Amminadab, sister of Naashon, to wife; and she bare him Nadab, and Abihu, Eleazar, and Ithamar.

24 And the sons of Korah; Assir, and Elkanah, and Abiasaph: these *are* the families of the Korhites.

25 And Eleazar Aaron's son took him *one* of the daughters of Putiel to wife; and she bare him Phinehas: these *are*

	the heads of the fathers of the Levites according to their families.
26	These *are* that Aaron and Moses, to whom the LORD said, Bring out the children of Israel from the land of Egypt according to their armies.
27	These *are* they which spoke to Pharaoh king of Egypt, to bring out the children of Israel from Egypt: these *are* that Moses and Aaron.
28	And it came to pass on the day *when* the LORD spoke unto Moses in the land of Egypt,
29	That the LORD spoke unto Moses, saying, I *am* the LORD: speak you unto Pharaoh king of Egypt all that I say unto you.
30	And Moses said before the LORD, Behold, I *am* of uncircumcised lips, and how shall Pharaoh listen to me?

This passage has to do with the two authorities by which Moses and Aaron went before Pharaoh. Moses was God's chosen one, while Aaron was merely the voice of the chosen one. They were both commissioned by God. Charged with an impossible task, they were to be God's voice.

But they had another authority. They were the children of Levi. The children of Israel. Their authority was of God, but it is also important to understand that the authority by which they spoke was as representatives of the children of Israel. They were not some foreign people with no bearing, and they were not a neutral 3rd party.

Islam's Muhammad claims he was sent as a prophet to the Jews and the Arabs. He was rejected by the Jews because he was not one of them. Believe it or not, genealogy has some importance. Notice here that Moses does not claim his Egyptian mother as his own. Rather, his Jewish blood, not his Egyptian heritage, gives him this second authority. It is undeniable to the Jews who he is. God has chosen one from among them. This the people of Israel could accept.

Dear God,

I am the child of those who raised me. I am one of the sinners who needed and continues to need your love. I am one of the sinners chosen by You. My charge from you is to share the power and wonder of the Good News of your great work, your sacrifice for us so that we may have life. I was chosen from among sinners so that they may accept me. That they too, might grasp this incredible truth in who You are. Lord, YOU chose me. Put me to work sharing Your love.

In Jesus name, Amen.

DAY #21
EXODUS 7:1-7

1   And the LORD said unto Moses, See, I have made you a god to Pharaoh: and Aaron your brother shall be your prophet.
2   You shall speak all that I command you: and Aaron your brother shall speak unto Pharaoh, that he send the children of Israel out of his land.
3   And I will harden Pharaoh's heart, and multiply my signs and my wonders in the land of Egypt.

4	But Pharaoh shall not hearken unto you, that I may lay my hand upon Egypt, and bring forth mine armies, *and* my people the children of Israel, out of the land of Egypt by great judgments.
5	And the Egyptians shall know that I *am* the LORD, when I stretch forth mine hand upon Egypt, and bring out the children of Israel from among them.
6	And Moses and Aaron did as the LORD commanded them, so did they.
7	And Moses *was* fourscore years old, and Aaron fourscore and three years old, when they spoke unto Pharaoh.

This marks the end of the second conversation Moses had with God. God tells them he keeps His promises. God also reminds them without saying, "I told you so." That he had said it would take time for Pharaoh would not to let them go easily. The scriptures clearly indicate that Moses is eighty years old and his brother Aaron is 83 at this time. Sadly in today's world, this is a time when we still revere our older generation, but we have begun to care for them. But Moses is still going strong at eighty! Aaron is also strong and has all his faculties. Moses and Aaron are not thought of as doddering old men but as men who are examples of how to live, men who have lived hard lives.

The key in the passage is, "Moses and Aaron did as the LORD commanded them," These men in their eighties made a meeting with the Pharaoh. Knowing that they would likely be killed if things did not work out well. But they scheduled or reserved this meeting without fear. They did this knowing God would tell them more of what to say and do.

Sometimes we need to listen to God. We want so much to have things now. We do not listen. We do not wait. We do not even act on our faith. We simply go about doing what we would normally do. We want to be people of faith but do not want to take the time to listen. This causes us to lose out sometimes. It can cause us to be wasteful of what we have. Simply doing what God wants of us and listening and waiting is not an easy task. Would you have been like Moses and Aaron and scheduled that appointment with a man who could easily cause your death while possessing great confidence in God's victory? Would you really?

Dear Lord Jesus,

I know that you provide for me. I know it is you who put a roof over my head and you who provide the income that allows me to get food. It is you who creates those opportunities for me to feed my children when my meager earnings are near nothing. Lord, how can I be so much less bold than Moses and his brother? How is it that I do not spend time trusting and waiting for your answers? I know who you are. I know what You have done for me. How dare I not act as you desire. How dare I not take the stand you desire that I take. Lord, help me see what you want me to do. Embolden me. Lord, strengthen my ability to seek your will and to listen to your guidance.

In Jesus name, Amen.

DAY #22
EXODUS 7:8-13

8   And the LORD spoke unto Moses and unto Aaron, saying,
9   When Pharaoh shall speak unto you, saying, Shew a miracle for you: then you shalt say unto Aaron, Take your rod, and cast *it* before Pharaoh, *and* it shall become a serpent.
10 And Moses and Aaron went in unto Pharaoh, and they did so as the LORD had commanded: and Aaron cast down his rod before Pharaoh, and before his servants, and it became a serpent.
11 Then Pharaoh also called the wise men and the sorcerers: now the magicians of Egypt, they also did in like manner with their enchantments.
12 For they cast down every man his rod, and they became serpents: but Aaron's rod swallowed up their rods.
13 And he hardened Pharaoh's heart, that he hearkened not unto them; as the LORD had said.

God speaks to Moses and Aaron for the third time; this is Moses' third encounter with God. This is not a conversation. God says do this, and Moses and Aaron obey. Every minute detail is prepared for them. God prepared them to turn the rod into a serpent as a sign to the Hebrews.

Pharaoh demands the sign. He is thinking of why he should listen to people whose God allowed them to be enslaved. They must have a puny god, Pharaoh thought.

Pharaoh has witnessed the rod-to-snake transformation. It is likely he heard of it when Moses and Aaron presented themselves to the Hebrew elders. Someone was likely a spy serving Pharaoh's men. This would be the explanation as to why so many priests could do the "magic act." But for Moses, this was not an act but a real and true thing. His rod snake swallowed theirs. Pharaoh is now questioning if this god of the slaves is such a puny god after all.

This one deed was enough to leave a powerful impression. But it hardly is what God called his wonders. Moses and Aaron knew this. It makes you wonder how they felt knowing this was the beginning of a long process with no idea how long it would be.

One of my pastors gave a sermon not long ago about trusting the process. Trusting that God was in control and *knowing* He would do what He has promised. Are you ready to trust the process at the beginning? It is not an easy thing.

Dear Lord Jesus,

You alone are in control of all that exists. You brought each little thing into existence. How can I not put my faith in You? Lord, I am not asking for patience. Lord, talk to me about the end of that process. Remind me of what You have at the end of the process. You have me in. I know that I am one You are not finished with yet. I know that You have planned a lot for me. Lord, I desire to be used by You to share Your word, to plant seeds, for Your harvest. Lord, I ask for encouragement. Please give me something that tells me You are working on something special for me.

In Jesus' name, Amen.

DAY #23
EXODUS 7:14-25

14 And the LORD said unto Moses, Pharaoh's heart *is* hardened, he refuses to let the people go.

15 Get you unto Pharaoh in the morning; lo, he goes out unto the water; and you shall stand by the river's brink against he come; and the rod which was turned to a serpent shall you take in your hand.

16 And you shall say unto him, The LORD God of the Hebrews has sent me unto you, saying, Let my people go, that they may serve me in the wilderness: and, behold, hitherto you would not hear.

17 Thus saith the LORD, In this you shalt know that I *am* the LORD: behold, I will smite with the rod that *is* in mine hand upon the waters which *are* in the river, and they shall be turned to blood.

18 And the fish that *is* in the river shall die, and the river shall stink; and the Egyptians shall loathe to drink of the water of the river.

19 And the LORD spoke unto Moses, Say unto Aaron, Take your rod, and stretch out your hand upon the waters of Egypt, upon their streams, upon their rivers, and upon their ponds, and upon all their pools of water, that they may become blood; and *that* there may be blood throughout all the land of Egypt, both in *vessels of* wood, and in *vessels of* stone.

20 And Moses and Aaron did so, as the LORD commanded; and he lifted up the rod, and smote the waters that *were* in the river, in the sight of Pharaoh, and in the sight of his servants; and all the waters that *were* in the river were turned to blood.

21 And the fish that *was* in the river died; and the river stank, and the Egyptians could not drink of the water of the river; and there was blood throughout all the land of Egypt.
22 And the magicians of Egypt did so with their enchantments: and Pharaoh's heart was hardened, neither did he hearken unto them; as the LORD had said.
23 And Pharaoh turned and went into his house, neither did he set his heart to this also.
24 And all the Egyptians digged round about the river for water to drink; for they could not drink of the water of the river.
25 And seven days were fulfilled, after that the LORD had smitten the river.

The wonders begin here. God's mighty wonder of turning water into blood. Many call this the first of the 10 plagues. But think of this as a wonder – a marvelous miracle created by God to show Pharaoh, the people of Egypt, and the Hebrew people who God is! Yes, the Hebrew people had to hear who he was again. They needed to be reminded.

Some might read this passage, laugh, and say that the Egyptian priests could do the same thing. Really? Did they change all the water in Egypt into blood by simply dipping the bottom of a rod into the water? The priests had to be scared. They had great control over the people. They could do just about anything they desired. But now, Moses and Aaron came before them. Last time, their rod turned into a snake and ate all of their snakes. This time their God went far beyond any trick or illusion. This god of the Hebrews dared to stretch forth his hand and change all the rivers, ponds, and more into the blood. The stench of the dead fish – the smell of the blood was more than they expected.

The people had to be begging Pharaoh for water. They had to be asking a lot of questions about what happened. How is it possible? Can a man do this? The answer is no, but to think of a god... no, not a god, THE GOD! What this means must have been ringing in their heads.

What would you say if you were there? Would you marvel at this wonder of God? Would you see this as a horrible plague? Would you see this as a sign God is acting on your behalf?

Dear Lord Jesus,

Help me Lord, to see Your hand in all that I do. Help me to see Your work and actions. Help me to see Your planning in action. Lord Jesus, I desire to be one who shares Your word with others. Use me. Empower me with your boldness as you did Moses and Aaron. Grant me the ability to share Your love with those who are angry and need You.

In Jesus name, Amen.

DAY #24
EXODUS 8:1-8

1   And the LORD spoke unto Moses, Go unto Pharaoh, and say unto him, Thus saith the LORD, Let my people go, that they may serve me.

2   And if you refuse to let *them* go, behold, I will smite all your borders with frogs:

3	And the river shall bring forth frogs abundantly, which shall go up and come into your house, and into your bedchamber, and upon your bed, and into the house of your servants, and upon your people, and into your ovens, and into your kneading troughs:
4	And the frogs shall come up both on you, and upon your people, and upon all your servants.
5	And the LORD spoke unto Moses, Say unto Aaron, Stretch forth your hand with your rod over the streams, over the rivers, and over the ponds, and cause frogs to come up upon the land of Egypt.
6	And Aaron stretched out his hand over the waters of Egypt; and the frogs came up, and covered the land of Egypt.
7	And the magicians did so with their enchantments, and brought up frogs upon the land of Egypt.
8	Then Pharaoh called for Moses and Aaron, and said, Intreat the LORD, that he may take away the frogs from me, and from my people; and I will let the people go, that they may do sacrifice unto the LORD.

The first wonder was scary – all the bodies of water in Egypt were turned to blood! This second one almost seems hilarious and very annoying. Who likes the idea of accidentally stepping on a frog? YUCK! Then who is getting any rest or sleep with these annoyances croaking and jumping on your bed? Try cooking with frogs jumping into the oven as you cook. Who wants a little of frogs with this or that?

But think about the last wonder. The water turned to blood should have killed most of the frogs, right? Frogs hibernate and burrow into the mud. They survived this wonder and multiplied incredibly. Could you take this for 2 days, how about 7? I find it interesting there is no counting of days here as to how long it took before Pharaoh called Moses begging for relief.

Sleep deprivation because of constant annoyances. Frogs were jumping on you all through the night. Would you have lasted long?

Dear Lord Jesus!

May Your greatness be seen in all the earth. My God is one of love. My God is one of humor! I can only picture someone laughing at the scene of frogs everywhere. Annoyances – something simple, yet frogs seem to be something boys love. God, you used even them! Lord, please use me to share Your great love. Direct me so I may share your wonders and so much more with those who do not yet know You.

In Jesus name, Amen.

DAY #25
EXODUS 8:9-15

9   And Moses said unto Pharaoh, Glory over me: when shall I intreat for you, and for your servants, and for your people, to destroy the frogs from you and your houses, *that* they may remain in the river only?

10   And he said, Tomorrow. And he said, *Be it* according to your word: that you may know that *there is* none like unto the LORD our God.

11   And the frogs shall depart from you, and from your houses, and from your servants, and from your people; they shall remain in the river only.

12   And Moses and Aaron went out from Pharaoh: and Moses cried unto the LORD because of the frogs which he had brought against Pharaoh.

13   And the LORD did according to the word of Moses; and the frogs died out of the houses, out of the villages, and out of the fields.

14   And they gathered them together upon heaps: and the land stank.

15   But when Pharaoh saw that there was respite, he hardened his heart, and hearkened not unto them; as the LORD had said.

Some people you meet are notorious complainers. They complain about this ache, that pain, and oh, the detail of it. Pharaoh is like them. Oh, the pain of frogs being everywhere! He can do nothing about it and complains to the man who can do everything about it. He has nothing to complain about when the pain is gone, so he acts to get something to complain about.

That is a pretty simple view of this. But look at verse 10. Moses has asked when he should ask God for relief. Pharaoh answers Tomorrow. This tells you that the frogs were an annoyance and an ever-present one. They were so annoying he could not sleep.

Verse 10 also has Moses stating, "Be it according to your word." Pharaoh does not realize it, but his choice of words is what is holding Egypt in bondage. Pharaoh does get that he has the power to set the Hebrew people free but has no idea that the words of Moses here are foreshadowing that God is not only listening to Pharaoh.

He is using those words to take appropriate action against him and the land of Egypt.

When the frogs are finally gone, when the stink is evidence of the demise of the frogs and evidence of there having been so many of them, so many that it seems impossible so many had come from their "life-giving river." Pharaoh acts like a spoiled child who always gets his way. He takes back his promise. He did not care that Moses could petition his God and that they received a time of relief. He only thinks of his own wants and needs. Something a toddler thinks of as they cry out, "I want this …" over and over when they think a tantrum will get them what they want.

Pharaoh says No once again. But God had told Moses that he would show them HIS wonders. Moses knew there would be more. These two wonders seemed huge but small for one reason. Pharaoh's magicians were able to do them. But God's actions were so vast and numerous that Pharaoh could not call on his magicians for help. Knowing what Moses knew, you have to wonder if Moses trusted Pharaoh to keep his word.

Do you see God's wonders in the painting that is a sunrise or a sunset? Moses must have been wondering what is coming next. Do you look at the world and ask the same question?

Dear Lord Jesus,

Please, Lord, open my eyes to your wonders about me. Help me to see the world through your eyes. Help me to see it with the love you have for us. Lord, may I see your hand in your mighty plans for a simple moment in my life. Lord, may I also be part of Your plans. Lord, please make me one of those You send out to share the glorious and great Good News of Your work on the cross.

In Jesus name, Amen.

DAY #26
EXODUS 8:16-19

16 And the LORD said unto Moses, Say unto Aaron, Stretch out your rod, and smite the dust of the land, that it may become lice throughout all the land of Egypt.
17 And they did so; for Aaron stretched out his hand with his rod, and smote the dust of the earth, and it became lice in man, and in beast; all the dust of the land became lice throughout all the land of Egypt.
18 And the magicians did so with their enchantments to bring forth lice, but they could not: so there were lice upon man, and upon beast.
19 Then the magicians said unto Pharaoh, This *is* the finger of God: and Pharaoh's heart was hardened, and he hearkened not unto them; as the LORD had said.

Imagine being beset by lice. You feel so gross. They get in your hair. They make you feel like itching all day long. You can do nothing to get them to leave except take medicine or shave yourself bald. If you're a woman, that will not happen during this wonder! A wonder the Egyptians called the finger of God.

You have to ask what made them say this. What was it about the fleas that made them call it the finger of God? Maybe it was how many suddenly formed and dispersed. Perhaps it was because they formed the shape of a finger and dispersed. But it was something they could not cheaply copy. It was something that they considered far beyond their ability, so much that it scared them.

When you look at the world today, do you look at it through fearful eyes when you see God's wonders, or do you look through eyes that proclaim God's glory? Are you fearful of what you see or hear, or are you stepping out in awe of God's wonder?

Dear Lord Jesus,

I can be a mighty clod, a fool. Yet I desire to see your work as a wonder. Lord, let me see your hand as wonders. Let me see your work as miracles wrought for us. Lord, you pain the very skies I so easily dismiss throughout the day. You show me so many wonders! Lord, use me. Use me so that I may share your wonders with others.

In Jesus name, Amen.

DAY #27
EXODUS 8:16-19

20   And the LORD said unto Moses, Rise up early in the morning, and stand before Pharaoh; lo, he cometh forth to the water; and say unto him, Thus said the LORD, Let my people go, that they may serve me.

21   Else, if you will not let my people go, behold, I will send swarms *of flies* upon you, and upon your servants, and upon your people, and into your houses: and the houses of the Egyptians shall be full of swarms *of flies*, and also the ground whereon they *are*.

22 And I will sever in that day the land of Goshen, in which my people dwell, that no swarms *of flies* shall be there; to the end you mayest know that I *am* the LORD in the midst of the earth.
23 And I will put a division between my people and your people: tomorrow shall this sign be.
24 And the LORD did so; and there came a grievous swarm *of flies* into the house of Pharaoh, and *into* his servants' houses, and into all the land of Egypt: the land was corrupted by reason of the swarm of flies.

This is the third wonder to hit Egypt. Flies are such an annoyance. They are tiresome, irksome, and so annoying that you feel compelled to swat them. But the abundance spoken of here speaks to significant sanitation issues and more. Verse 24 even states that "the land was corrupted."

Flies are seemingly bothersome insects but are also known for carrying diseases. Part of the significance of how they spread disease is that they cannot eat solid food; they vomit out onto something, and their vomit liquefies the item. Then they suck it up. Gross, right? Now consider where you see large amounts of flies and how they do not differentiate between bile, feces, and food.

Flies as an annoyance is one thing, but they bring with them so much that is dangerous. It is no wonder that the land was corrupted. In some areas, flies bite you. That would actually be them vomiting on you since they have no teeth. Yes, EWW GROSS!

Worse yet, being the Pharaoh and seeing that the Land of Goshen, where the Hebrew people lived, had no single fly plaguing them. What would the people think when they figured this out? What a wonder both the Hebrew and Egyptian people must have said as they observed the night and day difference.

How long would you be willing to put up with such an infestation? How long do you think it would be before the people complained to you about this if it happened that you were the leader?

Dear Lord Jesus!

Annoyances are things we want to live without. But you, Oh Lord, are essential for my life. I can not live a day without your love. Lord, use me to share these wonders and the wonder of your love for us.

In Jesus name, Amen

DAY #28
EXODUS 8:25-32

25   And Pharaoh called for Moses and for Aaron, and said, Go you, sacrifice to your God in the land.
26   And Moses said, It is not meet so to do; for we shall sacrifice the abomination of the Egyptians to the LORD our God: lo, shall we sacrifice the abomination of the Egyptians before their eyes, and will they not stone us?
27   We will go three days' journey into the wilderness, and sacrifice to the LORD our God, as he shall command us.
28   And Pharaoh said, I will let you go, that you may sacrifice to the LORD your God in the wilderness; only you shall not go very far away: intreat for me.

29   And Moses said, Behold, I go out from you, and I will intreat the LORD that the swarms *of flies* may depart from Pharaoh, from his servants, and from his people, to morrow: but let not Pharaoh deal deceitfully any more in not letting the people go to sacrifice to the LORD.

30   And Moses went out from Pharaoh, and intreated the LORD.

31   And the LORD did according to the word of Moses; and he removed the swarms *of flies* from Pharaoh, from his servants, and from his people; there remained not one.

32   And Pharaoh hardened his heart at this time also, neither would he let the people go.

Water into blood, Frogs, Fleas, Flies, what next? That has to be on Pharaoh's mind. Can it get worse? Pharaoh is so reluctant to free the Hebrew people that he seems to connect whatever success he has in not letting them go. Even though now he has seen that there is a definite problem in keeping them. When the flies came, no one in Goshen experienced the issue. They slaved in Egypt but returned to the area known as Goshen to sleep.

Pharaoh thinks he is the one in total control. He turns Moses's request to free his people to make a sacrifice into a personal request. He only approves of Moses going and making a sacrifice. He also only approves of a limited distance. This is an attempt to make Moses please him and not serve the God Moses says is telling him to let HIS people go.

Pharaoh gets what he wants. The immediate relief from the flies. But it comes with a cost for Pharaoh and the Egyptian people. The delay in Moses's return since he was to go about a day's journey away gave the people time to remember their comfort as slave owners. The cost would be to experience something worse than the last 4 Wonders that hit Egypt.

Comfort – it is a great feeling. But it can be a distracting place to be. If you are comfortable, will you grow? Will you desire to learn more? Oil-rich nations pay their citizens simply for living. They have no desire to learn and improve. Those who do usually leave the country. Are you in a place of comfort? If so, are you willing to step out of that place of comfort and stretch and grow? Do it today!

Dear Lord Jesus!

Help me to make better choices. Help me to stand tall for you. Guide me. Direct my steps so that I may be an example to others. Use me so that I may show others of your glory and wonders. Lord take me out of my comfort zone. Show me new ways to grow and become a better servant to you.

In Jesus name, Amen.

DAY #29
EXODUS 9:1-7

1   Then the LORD said unto Moses, Go in unto Pharaoh, and tell him, Thus saith the LORD God of the Hebrews, Let my people go, that they may serve me.
2   For if you refuse to let *them* go, and wilt hold them still,
3   Behold, the hand of the LORD is upon your cattle which *is* in the field, upon the horses, upon the asses, upon the

	camels, upon the oxen, and upon the sheep: *there shall be* a very grievous murrain.
4	And the LORD shall sever between the cattle of Israel and the cattle of Egypt: and there shall nothing die of all *that is* the children's of Israel.
5	And the LORD appointed a set time, saying, To morrow the LORD shall do this thing in the land.
6	And the LORD did that thing on the morrow, and all the cattle of Egypt died: but of the cattle of the children of Israel died not one.
7	And Pharaoh sent, and, behold, there was not one of the cattle of the Israelites dead. And the heart of Pharaoh was hardened, and he did not let the people go.

POWER. The great and living God is ALL-POWERFUL! He is OMNIPOTENT! Pharaoh has seen water change to blood, frogs, fleas, and flies by this point. God has shown Pharaoh only a tidbit of his ability. God has shown him his ability to manipulate water, frogs, and insects in some ways. Maybe this seemed minuscule to Pharaoh, but in truth, he had been warned by the changing of water into blood. Why do I say this? Because in the water to blood wonder, the atomic structure of the water changed. For the frogs, flies, and fleas, He created them out of nothing. The scientific name being *ex-nihilo*. Yet Pharaoh only saw what existed, not their creation. He saw this as manipulation.

Now we get to the death of cattle. Murrain, pronounced *Murr-in*, is archaic. We don't see this word used today. Dictionary. com defines the word as:

1. Veterinary Pathology. Any of various diseases of cattle, such as anthrax, foot-and-mouth disease, and Texas fever.

2. Obsolete. a plague or pestilence.

This definition shows that this word meant "pestilence," but today, it refers to a few very well-known biohazards. Anthrax is one of those items that causes fear. Its deadly grasp and deadly concoction are pretty much a guaranteed killer. Pharaoh may have missed that God had created insects out of nothing to show HIS power. So that Pharaoh only saw manipulation. But now, manipulation is happening on a much smaller scale that we call micro-biology. On top of this, God tells Pharaoh of the timing.

You would think that this wonder, this display of God's hand killing only the cattle owned by the Egyptians, should have been a wake-up call. Pharaoh can now no longer have beef. They will have to buy more or steal from the Hebrew people. How is this not enough of a display of God's power? How is that not enough to make Pharaoh grasp what must be done?

Death – stinks, literally. Especially when it is not disposed of quickly – Pharaoh saw that with the fish and the frogs' deaths. But cattle are massive in comparison. Why did he not see this?

Believe it or not, people whose hearts are hardened against God see only what they want and filter everything away that speaks of God's existence. They forsake knowledge of logic to lift up themselves and their limited viewpoint. Step back and take a look around yourself. Do you see God's hand in what is around you?

Dear Lord Jesus,

You were there from the beginning. By your hand, all that has been created exists through You. Your awesome incredible power is far beyond our grasp. You grasp the small details. You plan ahead for us. Lord, please use me. Use me that I may draw men unto you with nets like Peter, James, and John.

In Jesus name, Amen.

DAY #30
EXODUS 9:8-12

8   And the LORD said unto Moses and unto Aaron, Take to you handfuls of ashes of the furnace, and let Moses sprinkle it toward the heaven in the sight of Pharaoh.
9   And it shall become small dust in all the land of Egypt, and shall be a boil breaking forth *with* blains upon man, and upon beast, throughout all the land of Egypt.
10 And they took ashes of the furnace, and stood before Pharaoh; and Moses sprinkled it up toward heaven; and it became a boil breaking forth *with* blains upon man, and upon beast.
11 And the magicians could not stand before Moses because of the boils; for the boil was upon the magicians, and upon all the Egyptians.
12 And the LORD hardened the heart of Pharaoh, and he hearkened not unto them; as the LORD had spoken unto Moses.

Boils are painful pus-filled areas of infection on your body. The pain is caused by the constant pressure from the expanding amount of pus. GROSS – disgusting and, yes, painful.

The places where these horrible sores grow upon the body are also regions that would bring extreme discomfort. It's no surprise that the priests of the fake gods cannot stand.

This Wonder marks the first one to effect Pharaoh personally. For some people, things are not real unless they are personal. Everything that had happened was outside the body until now.

This time, God ends the Wonder of boils. His mercifulness does not let this continue. Maybe it is because Pharaoh actually begs God for relief in this state of painful torture from boils. A private call to the Hebrew God on his part would only reveal who God is to him alone. Imagine the surprise of Pharaoh when Moses arrives the next morning if this is the case.

Dear Lord Jesus,

You alone are God; besides you, there is no other! There is no one and no thing that can compare to You. Lord, strengthen me. Make me stronger so that I may stand boldly proclaiming who you are to others. Use me that I may awaken others to your holy presence at the door knocking on the doors of their hearts.

In Jesus name, Amen.

DAY #29
EXODUS 9:13-21

13   And the LORD said unto Moses, Rise up early in the morning, and stand before Pharaoh, and say unto him, Thus saith

the LORD God of the Hebrews, Let my people go, that they may serve me.

14   For I will at this time send all my plagues upon your heart, and upon your servants, and upon your people; that you may know that *there is* none like me in all the earth.

15   For now I will stretch out my hand, that I may smite you and your people with pestilence; and you shalt be cut off from the earth.

16   And in very deed for this *cause* have I raised you up, for to shew *in* you my power; and that my name may be declared throughout all the earth.

17   As yet you exalt yourself against my people, that you wilt not let them go?

18   Behold, to morrow about this time I will cause it to rain a very grievous hail, such as hath not been in Egypt since the foundation thereof even until now.

19   Send therefore now, *and* gather your cattle, and all that you have in the field; *for upon* every man and beast which shall be found in the field, and shall not be brought home, the hail shall come down upon them, and they shall die.

20   He that feared the word of the LORD among the servants of Pharaoh made his servants and his cattle flee into the houses:

21   And he that regarded not the word of the LORD left his servants and his cattle in the field.

This passage is intimately personal between God and Pharaoh, using Moses as his mouthpiece. He speaks to Pharaoh, warning and telling him that there is more to come so that Pharaoh will release HIS people. God even says that Pharaoh was born for this reason, that people may know who God is. That they may see His plagues,

His wonders and know that there is indeed only one God who is and reigns supreme. That ALL may know who God is throughout all the earth!

Pharaoh is given a choice that would preserve and keep people alive. He can now issue a warning that the God of the Hebrews will smite the land with hail and fire or watch his people and their existing cattle, albeit they must have just purchased them or done nothing and be removed by his own people. Pharaoh issues the warning. Making him a voice piece of the living God. He warns his people about the dangerous God of the Hebrew people who will smite the land in such a horrific manner that has never yet happened upon the earth.

Now, think about this, if you were told of some horrendous weather that had never yet existed, would you believe it was going to happen? How about if you had just seen water turned to blood, frogs, fleas, flies, and the death of your cattle? Pretty good examples to make you be cautious. You almost have to ask what it will take to wake this puny human up. God could simply smite him. That much is painfully obvious. But God has said that Pharaoh is here so that God can be known. Think about that. God even uses what is horrible for good!

Dear Lord Jesus,

How You love me so is a marvel. I am a sinner who does not deserve Your love. You loved me first! FIRST! Lord, You planned for me and continue to plan a great many things just for me. Your greatness is known to me. Use me as part of Your plans to share your love with others. Let me be Your beacon.

In Jesus name, Amen.

DAY #30
EXODUS 9:22-28

22   And the LORD said unto Moses, Stretch forth your hand toward heaven, that there may be hail in all the land of Egypt, upon man, and upon beast, and upon every herb of the field, throughout the land of Egypt.
23   And Moses stretched forth his rod toward heaven: and the LORD sent thunder and hail, and the fire ran along upon the ground; and the LORD rained hail upon the land of Egypt.
24   So there was hail, and fire mingled with the hail, very grievous, such as there was none like it in all the land of Egypt since it became a nation.
25   And the hail smote throughout all the land of Egypt all that *was* in the field, both man and beast; and the hail smote every herb of the field, and brake every tree of the field.
26   Only in the land of Goshen, where the children of Israel *were*, was there no hail.
27   And Pharaoh sent, and called for Moses and Aaron, and said unto them, I have sinned this time: the LORD *is* righteous, and I and my people *are* wicked.
28   Intreat the LORD (for *it is* enough) that there be no *more* mighty thunderings and hail; and I will let you go, and you shall stay no longer.

    This incredible miracle back then is something we can say we have some clue about today. The very concept of hot and ice sounds so opposite. Make it a fire, and it still is today. Today we can easily create Hot Ice at home. Sodium Acetate is a simple chemical composition with a wide variety of uses. But remember, this passage is not talking about hot ice; it's talking about FIRE and ICE mingled.

For most of us, this would be a great sign that God is on the throne, and we need to repent, beg his forgiveness AND obey whatever he asks of us. Would this act, this mighty Wonder of God, have you shaking in your boots, begging for mercy?

Pharaoh did call upon Moses to beg for relief. But did he feel a need to repent? No.

Dear Lord Jesus,

You molded the heavens and the earth. The very creation of time is part of your marvelous works. Who am I that You love me? You sent Your son to die in my place. My place…Lord, please never let me forget to put You first in my life. Never let me forget that You are always in control. Please do not let me be silent about Your great love.

In Jesus name, Amen.

DAY #31
EXODUS 9:29-35

29   And Moses said unto him, As soon as I am gone out of the city, I will spread abroad my hands unto the LORD; *and* the thunder shall cease, neither shall there be any more hail; that you may know how that the earth *is* the LORD'S.

30   But as for you and your servants, I know that you will not yet fear the LORD God.
31   And the flax and the barley was smitten: for the barley *was* in the ear, and the flax *was* bolled.
32   But the wheat and the rie were not smitten: for they *were* not grown up.
33   And Moses went out of the city from Pharaoh, and spread abroad his hands unto the LORD: and the thunders and hail ceased, and the rain was not poured upon the earth.
34   And when Pharaoh saw that the rain and the hail and the thunders were ceased, he sinned yet more, and hardened his heart, he and his servants.
35   And the heart of Pharaoh was hardened, neither would he let the children of Israel go; as the LORD had spoken by Moses.

Pharaoh has proven not to be what most would call a man of honor who keeps his word. It is no surprise at this point that Moses proclaims he will soon once again deny the very thing he promised. Still, Moses promises to raise his arms and end the relentless attack of fiery hail upon Egypt.

We have all heard of the desperate man who prays, promising God he will do his bidding if he is delivered or healed. When God heals or delivers the man from that horrible place, the man forgets his promises. He marks it up to pure chance rather than his petition to the living God. Do you see Pharaoh in this?

Pharaoh sins the moment the Wonder ceases. It's almost as if he knows Moses has this connection with God, and he does not care because all he cares about is pleasing himself. Why bother doing what the God of Moses asks if he can simply manipulate Moses to stop the actions of his God?

But now, Moses has proclaimed what Pharaoh will do before he does it. Pharaoh has to be wondering what is going on when he finds himself doing exactly what Moses said would happen. Is he, the manipulator, being manipulated by the God of Moses?

Sadly, those who think so highly of themselves take very little time to question themselves and their actions. Because they just can not be wrong – they believe. But we know WHO is never wrong. It is the Great "I am."

Dear Lord Jesus,

You are the great and living God. You alone are worthy of my praise. Lord, guide me that I may choose that which You desire for my life rather than what I desire. Help me to resist sinful desires. Strengthen me so that I may stand strong and be a man who stands for You. Embolden me that I may go beyond sharing my love of You and preach your endless love for us to those around me.

In Jesus name, Amen.

DAY #32
EXODUS 10:1-15

1   And the LORD said unto Moses, Go in unto Pharaoh: for I have hardened his heart, and the heart of his servants, that I might shew these my signs before him:
2   And that you may tell in the ears of your son, and of your son's son, what things I have wrought in Egypt, and my

signs which I have done among them; that you may know how that I *am* the LORD.

3   And Moses and Aaron came in unto Pharaoh, and said unto him, Thus saith the LORD God of the Hebrews, How long will you refuse to humble yourself before me? let my people go, that they may serve me.

4   Else, if you refuse to let my people go, behold, to morrow will I bring the locusts into your coast:

5   And they shall cover the face of the earth, that one cannot be able to see the earth: and they shall eat the residue of that which is escaped, which remains unto you from the hail, and shall eat every tree which grows for you out of the field:

6   And they shall fill your houses, and the houses of all your servants, and the houses of all the Egyptians; which neither your fathers, nor your fathers' fathers have seen, since the day that they were upon the earth unto this day. And he turned himself, and went out from Pharaoh.

7   And Pharaoh's servants said unto him, How long shall this man be a snare unto us? let the men go, that they may serve the LORD their God: know you not yet that Egypt is destroyed?

8   And Moses and Aaron were brought again unto Pharaoh: and he said unto them, Go, serve the LORD your God: *but* who *are* they that shall go?

9   And Moses said, We will go with our young and with our old, with our sons and with our daughters, with our flocks and with our herds will we go; for we *must hold* a feast unto the LORD.

10 And he said unto them, Let the LORD be so with you, as I will let you go, and your little ones: look [to it]; for evil *is* before you.

11 Not so: go now you *that are* men, and serve the LORD; for that you did desire. And they were driven out from Pharaoh's presence.

12 And the LORD said unto Moses, Stretch out your hand over the land of Egypt for the locusts, that they may come up upon the land of Egypt, and eat every herb of the land, *even* all that the hail hath left.

13 And Moses stretched forth his rod over the land of Egypt, and the LORD brought an east wind upon the land all that day, and all *that* night; *and* when it was morning, the east wind brought the locusts.

14 And the locusts went up over all the land of Egypt, and rested in all the coasts of Egypt: very grievous *were they*; before them there were no such locusts as they, neither after them shall be such.

15 For they covered the face of the whole earth, so that the land was darkened; and they did eat every herb of the land, and all the fruit of the trees which the hail had left: and there remained not any green thing in the trees, or in the herbs of the field, through all the land of Egypt.

It was curious how all plants were not set afire in the fiery hail wonder. It makes you ask questions as you think about that. But then they survived by the grace of God for this reason. God had plans to use them for this moment.

Pharaoh was warned, and his own people appear to have had enough of the work of the Hebrew God on them. They sound as if they would be happy to say good riddance. Pharaoh seems to listen to them but places restrictions on Moses' compliance with the requests of God. Actually, the restriction comes not on Moses and the Hebrew people but on the God of the Hebrews. This limit – is a statement of doubt and a statement of power. Pharaoh still believes that he is stronger than the God of the Hebrew people. After all, how could a powerful God allow His people to be slaves?

Pharaoh forgets that God plans ahead. He knows our needs before we ourselves know them. God allowed enslavement so it could be used to teach His people more about freedom. Only those who have had a loss of freedom truly know what it means to be free.

This limitation of Pharaoh is not small at all. It is made in the thought that if he lets only the women go, they will not return. If he let the children go, they would not return. But if he let the men go, they indeed would return. Not one of them would take the chance of leaving their wives and children in the hands of the Egyptians. Pharaoh thought he could make the Hebrew people stay. He thought they would be too subservient and stupid to understand this.

Yet this limit is not placed on the Hebrew people but on GOD. Because it is God who has demanded their freedom. God is using Moses and Aaron to come before Pharaoh and saying unto him, "Let my people go!"

The fact that the people know what a locust is and what they can do should not be lost here. It's possible in the time before Pharaoh called Moses back, he had men sent to look for signs of locusts anywhere in his kingdom or neighboring lands. Maybe that emboldened Pharaoh to limit God. But Pharaoh, for some reason, had not grasped God's ability to create things out of nothing (*ex nihilo*). Don't place limits on what God wants for you. When God asks something of you, don't limit what he asks of you. Give what he asks of you.

Dear Lord Jesus,

How great and mighty You are. You calm the seas, form mountains, and even know the number of hairs on our heads. Lord, your love is so uncompromising for us, You stand knocking at our doors relentlessly. You never stop asking us to come to You. You give us a choice. You do not force us to follow You. Lord, help me to share Your message of freedom. – Your message of choices vs. forced responses. Your message is indeed one of love.

In Jesus name, Amen.

DAY #33
EXODUS 10:16-20

16   Then Pharaoh called for Moses and Aaron in haste; and he said, I have sinned against the LORD your God, and against you.
17   Now therefore forgive, I pray you, my sin only this once, and intreat the LORD your God, that he may take away from me this death only.
18   And he went out from Pharaoh, and intreated the LORD.
19   And the LORD turned a mighty strong west wind, which took away the locusts, and cast them into the Red sea; there remained not one locust in all the coasts of Egypt.
20   But the LORD hardened Pharaoh's heart, so that he would not let the children of Israel go.

Pharaoh begs Moses to forgive his sin against him and his God. This is a significant step for Pharaoh to recognize that sin exists and that he is fallible. He can make mistakes; He can do that which is wrong. Pharaohs were raised as princes who could do no wrong. They would become gods. Yet, this god-man Pharaoh now has seen that he is sinful in the sight of the Hebrew people. But has he recognized that he sinned against God? No. At no time has he begged for forgiveness from God. At no time is the God of the Hebrew people recognized personally by Pharaoh. Pharaoh says, "the Lord your God." He talks about begging that death be removed as if he is asking for a nightmare to end. After all, when you wake from a nightmare, the world is set right again. Egypt was a land of plenty. Its wealth was overwhelming. Its harvest was so great that people came to them when they needed food. But now .... Now the crops are eaten. There is a threat of death by starvation if this continues.

Moses does go out and petitions God as Pharaoh requested. In some sense, Pharaoh's current nightmare is over. He must have felt elated as the wind picked up the roaches, sweeping them back to wherever they came from in his mind.

The locusts came from no place. The East wind brought them. Then a West wind is used to get rid of them. They are returned to nothing. This is a supernatural wind, for in a normal wind, locusts would fall to the ground at random, constantly having to be scooped up again and again.

How often do we not see the true big picture that God is in control? How often do we get some sense of worry and beg God to take care of a problem and not see how He is already doing that for us? We need to pray. We need to turn to God. We must be on our knees seeking HIS will, not our own as Pharaoh.

Dear Lord Jesus,

My sins---they are against You. They deserve punishment. Yet You, Lord, went to the cross to pay that price for me. You shed Your blood for me. Help me, Lord, to see the bigger picture of your mighty work. Help me to see that You are indeed the one in control. Lead me to become one who sees more and more reasons to praise Your holy name. I beg of You that you use this to draw others to You.

In Jesus name, Amen.

DAY #34
EXODUS 10:21-29

21   And the LORD said unto Moses, Stretch out your hand toward heaven, that there may be darkness over the land of Egypt, even darkness *which* may be felt.

22   And Moses stretched forth his hand toward heaven; and there was a thick darkness in all the land of Egypt three days:

23   They saw not one another, neither rose any from his place for three days: but all the children of Israel had light in their dwellings.

24   And Pharaoh called unto Moses, and said, Go you, serve the LORD; only let your flocks and your herds be stayed: let your little ones also go with you.

25   And Moses said, You must give us also sacrifices and burnt offerings, that we may sacrifice unto the LORD our God.

26   Our cattle also shall go with us; there shall not an hoof be left behind; for thereof must we take to serve the LORD our

	God; and we know not with what we must serve the LORD, until we come thither.
27	But the LORD hardened Pharaoh's heart, and he would not let them go.
28	And Pharaoh said unto him, Get you from me, take heed to yourself, see my face no more; for in *that* day you see my face you shall die.
29	And Moses said, You have spoken well, I will see your face again no more.

This wonder is one of the scariest so far. A darkness so dark it can be felt. So dark that not one Egyptian can find another. So dark it compels each one not to move. So dark it imprisons. For three days, they starve themselves, and Bodily functions occur where they are because the darkness they feel holds them there. Yet God took care of HIS chosen people. Light resided in their homes. Light without a lamp. Light without a source—or a known source. That light was from God, so these could have been angels.

People who are afraid of the dark reading this should thank God that Light overtakes darkness 100 percent of the time. We serve the creator of light itself – Jesus (John 1:1-3)! The light was created before the sun was created (Genesis 1:3-4).

Pharaoh here still thinks he can restrict or limit the requests of Moses without consequence. Think like a leader of a vast amount of people. Think of them like your army. An army travels on its stomach. What happens if you take a large amount of people someplace without any food? It is one thing for you to live on faith, knowing God will provide, but to start the journey of leading a group, many need to see a starting point. They need to know the ending point.

Pharaoh also has in the back of his mind the sorry state of his people at this point. The Egyptian crops have gone. Most of their cattle are dead. They are surviving based on their storage of surplus food. Pharaoh may have planned this answer thinking he could simply walk in and take what was theirs while they were giving this sacrifice.

When Moses says no, Pharaoh does not seem ready for that response. His military had not eaten for three days. He, himself, had to be ravenous. They were no match for the Hebrew people in their current state. How dare Moses say "NO!" Pharaoh responds by issuing a death threat.

Pharaoh has to be double angered that Moses responded without any fear. Moses knows God will take care of him. Moses responds with kind words complimenting his speech.

Dear Lord Jesus,

Lord, let me stand where you plant me. Let me not give in when offers of compromise come in for me to move off my stand in Your Word. Open my eyes to see the dangers of such answers. Lord, comfort me even when I think I stand alone so I may more firmly serve you than ever. Lord, use that boldness and chance to stand for what You desire to draw others to You.

In Jesus name, Amen.

DAY #35
EXODUS 11:1-10

1   And the LORD said unto Moses, Yet will I bring one plague *more* upon Pharaoh, and upon Egypt; afterwards he will let you go hence: when he shall let *you* go, he shall surely thrust you out hence altogether.

2   Speak now in the ears of the people, and let every man borrow of his neighbour, and every woman of her neighbour, jewels of silver, and jewels of gold.

3   And the LORD gave the people favour in the sight of the Egyptians. Moreover the man Moses *was* very great in the land of Egypt, in the sight of Pharaoh's servants, and in the sight of the people.

4   And Moses said, Thus saith the LORD, About midnight will I go out into the midst of Egypt:

5   And all the firstborn in the land of Egypt shall die, from the firstborn of Pharaoh that sit upon his throne, even unto the firstborn of the maidservant that *is* behind the mill; and all the firstborn of beasts.

6   And there shall be a great cry throughout all the land of Egypt, such as there was none like it, nor shall be like it any more.

7   But against any of the children of Israel shall not a dog move his tongue, against man or beast: that you may know how that the LORD does put a difference between the Egyptians and Israel.

8   And all these your servants shall come down unto me, and bow down themselves unto me, saying, Get you out, and all the people that follow you: and after that I will go out. And he went out from Pharaoh in a great anger.

9   And the LORD said unto Moses, Pharaoh shall not listen unto you; that my wonders may be multiplied in the land of Egypt.

10   And Moses and Aaron did all these wonders before Pharaoh: and the LORD hardened Pharaoh's heart, so that he would not let the children of Israel go out of his land.

This plague – this wonder is both the most horrible and an extremely scary display of God's power. Nine times God warned Pharaoh who HE was and what HE could do. Nine times Pharaoh dismissed God as if he was a servant to do the bidding of Pharaoh. It is not until Pharaoh threatens to kill God's messenger that this ... this plague of death is unleashed.

This plague is not announced to Pharaoh. God does not send Moses to share with Pharaoh of the coming terror.

Why the firstborn? There is something about the firstborn that resonates with the parents. They go through many firsts with their parents, from changing diapers to breastfeeding to their first days in school, first getting married, and first doing so many things. Parents hold these things in their hearts. It does not mean being born second or 12th, is any less important. But you learn from doing things the first time. That makes it precious.

God says this will not happen again, that such a thing as the death of the firstborn shall not happen. In all the time since, no disease, no pestilence has shown any ability to biotarget those born first.

God knows YOU! He knows your birth order; He knows everything about you. He knows your nationality, he knows how many hairs are on your head – or not.

If God knows YOU so personally, isn't He worth giving your all to?

Dear Lord Jesus,

Your work and wonder are so awesome. They start each day with a painting of the sky. They end each day with dancing stars you put in their place. You plan for me. You make wonders happen that I may never know about only to make my life better. You allow me to go through hardships to mold me into a better me. Lord use this person you have molded and shaped. Use me to draw others to you.

In Jesus name, Amen.

DAY #36
EXODUS 12:1-13

1 And the LORD spake unto Moses and Aaron in the land of Egypt, saying,
2 This month *shall be* unto you the beginning of months: it *shall be* the first month of the year to you.
3 Speak you unto all the congregation of Israel, saying, In the tenth *day* of this month they shall take to them every man a lamb, according to the house of *their* fathers, a lamb for an house:
4 And if the household be too little for the lamb, let him and his neighbour next unto his house take *it* according to the number of the souls; every man according to his eating shall make your count for the lamb.

5	Your lamb shall be without blemish, a male of the first year: you shall take *it* out from the sheep, or from the goats:
6	And you shall keep it up until the fourteenth day of the same month: and the whole assembly of the congregation of Israel shall kill it in the evening.
7	And they shall take of the blood, and strike *it* on the two side posts and on the upper door post of the houses, wherein they shall eat it.
8	And they shall eat the flesh in that night, roast with fire, and unleavened bread; *and* with bitter *herbs* they shall eat it.
9	Eat not of it raw, nor sodden at all with water, but roast *with* fire; his head with his legs, and with the purtenance thereof.
10	And you shall let nothing of it remain until the morning; and that which remains of it until the morning you shall burn with fire.
11	And thus shall you eat it; *with* your loins girded, your shoes on your feet, and your staff in your hand; and you shall eat it in haste: it *is* the LORD'S passover.
12	For I will pass through the land of Egypt this night, and will smite all the firstborn in the land of Egypt, both man and beast; and against all the gods of Egypt I will execute judgment: I *am* the LORD.
13	And the blood shall be to you for a token upon the houses where you *are*: and when I see the blood, I will pass over you, and the plague shall not be upon you to destroy *you*, when I smite the land of Egypt.

Chapter 11 talks about the plague being immediate. But Chapter 12 talks about this being days away. That appears confusing until you know that this chapter starts with the word spake and that the Hebrew scholars Jamison, Fausset, and Brown explain that this means "had spoken." God had spoken to his people previously. Chapter 11 is what Moses was to say to Pharaoh. Moses was already told to say what is in this chapter to his brethren, God's chosen, the Hebrew people.

They had about four days to prep for this horror. Moses heard this message about the 10th of the month. The Israelites are told that each family must take a lamb without blemish and separate it from the flock for four days. On that day, they are to kill the lamb in the evening. At this time, it meant about 3 pm. Then they had two more immediate things to do. 1. Take the blood from the lamb and paint the doorposts of their home and upper the post. 2. Cook the lamb.

That night they were to eat the lamb prepared to travel. They were to be ready. They were to be ready to leave in the morning. God was telling them, on this day, I will deliver you.

Can you imagine being told that something like deliverance would come to you on a specific date and time after a period of slavery so long your family could not remember ever being free? There were stories of life before slavery. But now, this living God tells them to prepare. On this particular day at this particular time, you will be leaving the bondage you have been held in.

They saw 9 wonderful miracles upon the land. They say how God separated them. Would this not be an incredible teaching tool for God to be listened to when he says, "On this day, you will leave." Who would question him, then? Can you imagine the excitement of eating that last meal? It would not have been one of fear of the angel of death racing about; it would have been one of excitement and promise! WE ARE LEAVING TOMORROW, was racing through their heads!

Dear Lord Jesus,

How much you plan for us always amazes me. You will even warn us or prepare us for things to come. Lord, you fill our tummies with Joy when evils surround us. You give us reason to praise You when sorrows abound. You are a motivational speaker! You encourage when things seem impossible. Lord, help me think about these things when all seems wrong around me. Use me that I may stand, if even alone, just for You!

In Jesus name, Amen.

DAY #37
EXODUS 12:14-28

14   And this day shall be unto you for a memorial; and you shall keep it a feast to the LORD throughout your generations; you shall keep it a feast by an ordinance for ever.

15   Seven days shall you eat unleavened bread; even the first day you shall put away leaven out of your houses: for whosoever eats leavened bread from the first day until the seventh day, that soul shall be cut off from Israel.

16   And in the first day *there shall be* an holy convocation, and in the seventh day there shall be an holy convocation to you; no manner of work shall be done in them, save *that* which every man must eat, that only may be done of you.

17   And you shall observe *the feast of* unleavened bread; for in this selfsame day have I brought your armies out of the land of Egypt: therefore shall you observe this day in your generations by an ordinance for ever.

18 In the first *month*, on the fourteenth day of the month at even, you shall eat unleavened bread, until the one and twentieth day of the month at even.

19 Seven days shall there be no leaven found in your houses: for whosoever eats that which is leavened, even that soul shall be cut off from the congregation of Israel, whether he be a stranger, or born in the land.

20 You shall eat nothing leavened; in all your habitations shall you eat unleavened bread.

21 Then Moses called for all the elders of Israel, and said unto them, Draw out and take you a lamb according to your families, and kill the passover.

22 And you shall take a bunch of hyssop, and dip *it* in the blood that *is* in the bason, and strike the lintel and the two side posts with the blood that *is* in the bason; and none of you shall go out at the door of his house until the morning.

23 For the LORD will pass through to smite the Egyptians; and when he sees the blood upon the lintel, and on the two side posts, the LORD will pass over the door, and will not suffer the destroyer to come in unto your houses to smite *you*.

24 And you shall observe this thing for an ordinance to you and to your sons for ever.

25 And it shall come to pass, when you be come to the land which the LORD will give you, according as he hath promised, that you shall keep this service.

26 And it shall come to pass, when your children shall say unto you, What mean you by this service?

27 That you shall say, It *is* the sacrifice of the LORD'S passover, who passed over the houses of the children of Israel in Egypt, when he smote the Egyptians, and delivered our houses. And the people bowed the head and worshipped.

28 And the children of Israel went away, and did as the LORD had commanded Moses and Aaron, so did they.

If the timeline here is what it seems to be, Moses told the elders to separate the lambs for the Passover before the darkness hit. The darkness comes upon them, and the sheep are separated until the end of the darkness. Then shortly after, Moses tells the people it is time for the Passover sacrifice.

Can you imagine being told to brush blood on the doorway of your house or apartment to ensure your family's safety? Can you imagine not doing it after seeing the light in your house when darkness was everywhere just a short time before? Next, all you have to do is cook the lamb and get ready to go.

Sounds simple, right? It took all of these wonders to get all of the Hebrew people to believe. How many times had they been told something would happen, and it did? How many times had they seen incredible miracles? All to push them to be obedient on this day.

The ritual of remembrance is not shared with the elders at this time. It was not important until the anniversary approached. No Hebrew would forget who they were and what they needed to do this day. NOT ONE!

They all would be made ready for an incredible adventure in the morning. Think about this. Some of them are probably packed for the four days! For three days, they could only pack what was inside their home. The borrowed jewels and more were done previously. Carts could have been hitched in the morning. Anything needed for travel must have been done in the morning. Nothing was being done at night. No one dared step outside.

Dear Lord Jesus!

How is it you are so patient and plan so wonderfully for our stubbornness? How can we ever hope to grasp your vastness and power when you do so much just for us? Every little step in your plan to get the Hebrew people out of Egypt had a purpose. Lord, please include me in your plans. Use me to plant seeds of your love.

In Jesus name, Amen.

DAY #38
EXODUS 12:29-42

29 And it came to pass, that at midnight the LORD smote all the firstborn in the land of Egypt, from the firstborn of Pharaoh that sat on his throne unto the firstborn of the captive that *was* in the dungeon; and all the firstborn of cattle.
30 And Pharaoh rose up in the night, he, and all his servants, and all the Egyptians; and there was a great cry in Egypt; for *there was* not a house where *there was* not one dead.
31 And he called for Moses and Aaron by night, and said, Rise up, *and* get you forth from among my people, both you and the children of Israel; and go, serve the LORD, as you have said.
32 Also take your flocks and your herds, as you have said, and be gone; and bless me also.
33 And the Egyptians were urgent upon the people, that they might send them out of the land in haste; for they said, We *be* all dead *men*.

34	And the people took their dough before it was leavened, their kneading troughs being bound up in their clothes upon their shoulders.
35	And the children of Israel did according to the word of Moses; and they borrowed of the Egyptians jewels of silver, and jewels of gold, and raiment:
36	And the LORD gave the people favour in the sight of the Egyptians, so that they lent unto them *such things as they required.* And they spoiled the Egyptians.
37	And the children of Israel journeyed from Rameses to Succoth, about six hundred thousand on foot *that were* men, beside children.
38	And a mixed multitude went up also with them; and flocks, and herds, *even* very much cattle.
39	And they baked unleavened cakes of the dough which they brought forth out of Egypt, for it was not leavened; because they were thrust out of Egypt, and could not tarry, neither had they prepared for themselves any victual.
40	Now the sojourning of the children of Israel, who dwelt in Egypt, *was* four hundred and thirty years.
41	And it came to pass at the end of the four hundred and thirty years, even the selfsame day it came to pass, that all the hosts of the LORD went out from the land of Egypt.
42	It *is* a night to be much observed unto the LORD for bringing them out from the land of Egypt: this *is* that night of the LORD to be observed of all the children of Israel in their generations.

Can you imagine Moses telling you, that you would be leaving and then going through the ten wonders? Only a few days ago, Moses gave this strange order about killing a lamb and placing the blood on the doorpost. But you did it because of the incredible things you had seen happen. You feared what would happen if you chose to disobey. This time he said not only be ready but put on your travel clothes. You go to bed in them. The manner and approach with which this was announced make you feel some incredible sense of urgency. You feel inside you that you will be leaving when you get up. Hoping you will not be disappointed. Then something wakes you. It's not the cries of grief coming from the Egyptians. It is cries of excitement. "RISE UP! WE ARE LEAVING NOW!"

Yesterday you packed everything you would take with you. Your bundles are ready; you race out to gather your beasts of burden that will carry your bundles and your family. The cry of FREEDOM rings in your ears. After 430 years, that very night, you are being freed.

You watch the excitement in your children's eyes as they come out, one by one, some barely woken. Your wife brings out the bread she had made ready for the next day. It has not risen, and she looks a little disappointed in it, even though she had been told this would happen. It's a happy, sad moment for her. God kept his promise, but she enjoys making her family happy with her cooking and baking talents, this food would not be allowed to go to waste. She brings it along, also.

Do you feel the real excitement and wonder about what is to come, knowing all that was bondage is being left behind?

Dear Lord Jesus,

You keep your promises. You delivered the Hebrew people from bondage. You, oh Lord, are the great creator of so many wonders. Your plans are perfect! You worked out every detail to perfection. Lord, use me in your plans to share your love. Let me share that incredible best of all miracles – your work on the cross.

In Jesus name, Amen.

DAY #39
EXODUS 12:43-51

43   And the LORD said unto Moses and Aaron, This *is* the ordinance of the passover: There shall no stranger eat thereof:
44   But every man's servant that is bought for money, when you have circumcised him, then shall he eat thereof.
45   A foreigner and an hired servant shall not eat thereof.
46   In one house shall it be eaten; you shalt not carry forth ought of the flesh abroad out of the house; neither shall you break a bone thereof.
47   All the congregation of Israel shall keep it.
48   And when a stranger shall sojourn with you, and will keep the passover to the LORD, let all his males be circumcised, and then let him come near and keep it; and he shall be as one that is born in the land: for no uncircumcised person shall eat thereof.
49   One law shall be to him that is homeborn, and unto the stranger that sojourns among you.
50   Thus did all the children of Israel; as the LORD commanded Moses and Aaron, so did they.
51   And it came to pass the selfsame day, *that* the LORD did bring the children of Israel out of the land of Egypt by their armies.

If the Hebrew people did not know how they were seen by God as separate from others, set apart, and chosen, they should know now. Everything God did for them set them apart. God says here that he is willing to graft "strangers" into them. But they have to be willing to undergo circumcision. A bloody painful procedure. That would leave a man groaning in pain. This is usually done on babies. The memory of this is forgotten. Today we have anesthetics. We can dull the pain or put you to sleep—but not so for them.

Not many would choose to join, knowing they would have to endure such a hardship. Even today, if it were a requirement to believe in Christ, it would force many not to follow Christ. The good thing is that the gift of salvation was freely given. We are freely grafted into the vine by the shed blood of Christ. There is no action we can do to earn it.

Dear Lord Jesus,

I thank and praise you Lord, for your love of us. Like the Jews, you separate us from the world. You place your claim of "mine" upon us. You desire that we should honor you by more than our words. That our deeds should match our words. You desire our hearts more than our actions. Lord, mold me and make me into someone who shares your love.

In Jesus name, Amen.

DAY #40
EXODUS 13:1-16

1   And the LORD spake unto Moses, saying,
2   Sanctify unto me all the firstborn, whatsoever opens the womb among the children of Israel, *both* of man and of beast: it *is* mine.
3   And Moses said unto the people, Remember this day, in which you came out from Egypt, out of the house of bondage; for by strength of hand the LORD brought you out from this *place*: there shall no leavened bread be eaten.
4   This day came you out in the month Abib.
5   And it shall be when the LORD shall bring you into the land of the Canaanites, and the Hittites, and the Amorites, and the Hivites, and the Jebusites, which he sware unto your fathers to give you, a land flowing with milk and honey, that you shalt keep this service in this month.
6   Seven days you shalt eat unleavened bread, and in the seventh day *shall be* a feast to the LORD.
7   Unleavened bread shall be eaten seven days; and there shall no leavened bread be seen with you, neither shall there be leaven seen with you in all your quarters.
8   And you shalt shew your son in that day, saying, *This is done* because of that *which* the LORD did unto me when I came forth out of Egypt.
9   And it shall be for a sign unto you upon your hand, and for a memorial between your eyes, that the LORD'S law may be in your mouth: for with a strong hand hath the LORD brought you out of Egypt.
10 You shalt therefore keep this ordinance in his season from year to year.

11   And it shall be when the LORD shall bring you into the land of the Canaanites, as he sware unto you and to your fathers, and shall give it you,
12   That you shalt set apart unto the LORD all that opens the matrix, and every firstling that comes of a beast which you have; the males *shall be* the LORD'S.
13   And every firstling of an ass you shalt redeem with a lamb; and if you wilt not redeem it, then you shalt break his neck: and all the firstborn of man among your children shalt you redeem.
14   And it shall be when your son asks you in time to come, saying, What *is* this? that you shalt say unto him, By strength of hand the LORD brought us out from Egypt, from the house of bondage:
15   And it came to pass, when Pharaoh would hardly let us go, that the LORD slew all the firstborn in the land of Egypt, both the firstborn of man, and the firstborn of beast: therefore I sacrifice to the LORD all that opens the matrix, being males; but all the firstborn of my children I redeem.
16   And it shall be for a token upon your hand, and for frontlets between your eyes: for by strength of hand the LORD brought us forth out of Egypt.

There are some important lessons here. God freed the Hebrew people and did not want them to ever forget it. He did so by showing His might and power that they may believe. God also points out that the firstborn belongs to him. We owe to God our first fruits. Without this blessing, there is no second. God institutes the ritual known as the Passover. This meal has traditions and family rituals that all relate to God's deliverance of them.

God places emphasis on unleavened bread. He repeats this part. Leaven is symbolically portraying sin. There should be no sin as you remember the greatness of God for what he has done for you. To honor God in the act of thanksgiving, which is what the Passover meal is, you should not sin. Think of leaven like yeast, it affects whatever it gets into. It causes a change. Sin does this, and it also darkens the soul.

God loves us all. He desires to protect us; He loves us more than we can comprehend because he gives us free will. We can choose what we want to do, even if it is a bad choice. Parents are stuck watching their children make choices. It is hard to watch sometimes, especially when they make wrong choices. Strangely enough, this is one of the reasons parents become good prayer warriors. There is no one better for a parent to beg and plead from than God when it concerns their children.

Dear Lord Jesus,

Lord, you deliver me and those I love from so many reasons to feel sad. It is hard to even grasp the fullness of it. Lord, let me not forget the things which you have done for me. You died for me. You gave up all so that I may live eternally. What am I? I am a person of sinful desires. Lord, purify me so that my desires go to that which is good and right in Your eyes. Use me, Lord, that I may show others the great love You have shown me.

In Jesus name, Amen.

DAY #41
EXODUS 13:17-22

17　And it came to pass, when Pharaoh had let the people go, that God led them not *through* the way of the land of the Philistines, although that *was* near; for God said, Lest peradventure the people repent when they see war, and they return to Egypt:

18　But God led the people about, *through* the way of the wilderness of the Red sea: and the children of Israel went up harnessed out of the land of Egypt.

19　And Moses took the bones of Joseph with him: for he had straitly sworn the children of Israel, saying, God will surely visit you; and you shall carry up my bones away hence with you.

20　And they took their journey from Succoth, and encamped in Etham, in the edge of the wilderness.

21　And the LORD went before them by day in a pillar of a cloud, to lead them the way; and by night in a pillar of fire, to give them light; to go by day and night:

22　He took not away the pillar of the cloud by day, nor the pillar of fire by night, [from] before the people.

The Hebrew people had been slaves for a long time. Still, it is possible some may have known the direction home. Their direction was not the fastest way, but it was the way God wanted. Who were they to argue with, the one who delivered them from slavery? None of them could have missed the pillar of cloud by day and the pillar of fire by night. There must have been an incredible sense of urgency to go. A need for flight. Something that told them not to stop. Then the great feeling that their deliverer was with them. This

God who took them from their slavery did more than simply free them. He guided their footsteps.

Are you following the path God sets before you? It is not emblazoned with the pillar of fire leading the way in the darkness, but there is a way that God has set for you. When you find that path, you will know. There is something completely satisfying in serving the living God on the path he has set for you.

Dear Lord Jesus,

Help me to seek after your will. Help me choose what You want for my life vs. what I desire. Help me place Your word in my heart that I may make the choices I need each day. Help me choose what is right and good, without knowing that it is such a choice, but a choice that You would have me make. Lord, use me so that I may also draw others to you.

In Jesus name, Amen.

DAY #42
EXODUS 14:1-14

1   And the LORD spake unto Moses, saying,
2   Speak unto the children of Israel, that they turn and encamp before Pihahiroth, between Migdol and the sea, over against Baalzephon: before it shall you encamp by the sea.
3   For Pharaoh will say of the children of Israel, They *are* entangled in the land, the wilderness hath shut them in.

4	And I will harden Pharaoh's heart, that he shall follow after them; and I will be honoured upon Pharaoh, and upon all his host; that the Egyptians may know that I *am* the LORD. And they did so.
5	And it was told the king of Egypt that the people fled: and the heart of Pharaoh and of his servants was turned against the people, and they said, Why have we done this, that we have let Israel go from serving us?
6	And he made ready his chariot, and took his people with him:
7	And he took six hundred chosen chariots, and all the chariots of Egypt, and captains over every one of them.
8	And the LORD hardened the heart of Pharaoh king of Egypt, and he pursued after the children of Israel: and the children of Israel went out with an high hand.
9	But the Egyptians pursued after them, all the horses *and* chariots of Pharaoh, and his horsemen, and his army, and overtook them encamping by the sea, beside Pihahiroth, before Baalzephon.
10	And when Pharaoh drew nigh, the children of Israel lifted up their eyes, and, behold, the Egyptians marched after them; and they were sore afraid: and the children of Israel cried out unto the LORD.
11	And they said unto Moses, Because *there were* no graves in Egypt, hast you taken us away to die in the wilderness? wherefore hast you dealt thus with us, to carry us forth out of Egypt?
12	*Is* not this the word that we did tell you in Egypt, saying, Let us alone, that we may serve the Egyptians? For *it had been* better for us to serve the Egyptians, than that we should die in the wilderness.
13	And Moses said unto the people, Fear not, stand still, and see the salvation of the LORD, which he will shew to you

14 > to day: for the Egyptians whom you have seen to day, you shall see them again no more for ever.
>
> 14 The LORD shall fight for you, and you shall hold your peace.

As God told him to do, Moses warned the people that Pharaoh was coming. The comment on the wilderness shutting them in is actually a reference to them being in the Sinai Peninsula and not having a way out. The God of the Hebrews had led them in the form of a cloud by day and fire by night. They were directed to that spot. God had put them exactly where he wanted them. He wanted them to be seen by Pharaoh and his coming 600 chariots. That number may seem large to some, but in truth, it is a very small number of chariots, considering the size of armies.

Moses, full of confidence, sees the fear in the people when they see the chariots coming. Even though God had said this was coming, the people became fearful. It is almost as if they do not grasp the power and vastness of their God that brought them out of slavery.

Yet Moses remains confident when the army of chariots can be seen in the distance. The reason he stays strong in faith is his constant talks with the living God. He has seen the impossible become a reality, just as every other Israelite. What sets him apart are his talks with God. His statement, "THE LORD SHALL FIGHT FOR YOU. HOLD YOUR PEACE," is a bold proclamation that holds back a mob mentality of panic and chaos.

How many times in our lives would things have gotten better if we simply realized that God would fight for us and remain calm? Good leaders have poise. They do not lead us down a rabbit hole of panic and fear. They stand ready to fight on. Americans, in general, are pretty much the same also. Our culture tells us to fight on. It tells us not to accept fear or panic as the answer but to find another viable answer. The truth about this is our Christian history. Standing tall when all seems lost is not something unheard of in American history. It is seen in the Alamo. It is seen in so much of our history. It is the very reason many inventions have been made. GOD SHALL FIGHT FOR YOU. Keep that in your brain. Keep that in your core. For our God is able to do the impossible!

Dear Lord Jesus,

Lord, please embolden me. Help me to stand when others seem filled with panic. Help me to be the beacon of light that shines a path on the light of Your perfection. Help me to be the one who stands pointing the way to You when all seems lost. Help me to be the one who calmly says, "God shall fight for you."

In Jesus name, Amen.

DAY #43
EXODUS 14:15-22

15   And the LORD said unto Moses, Wherefore criest you unto me? speak unto the children of Israel, that they go forward:
16   But lift you up your rod, and stretch out your hand over the sea, and divide it: and the children of Israel shall go on dry *ground* through the midst of the sea.
17   And I, behold, I will harden the hearts of the Egyptians, and they shall follow them: and I will get me honour upon

	Pharaoh, and upon all his host, upon his chariots, and upon his horsemen.
18	And the Egyptians shall know that I *am* the LORD, when I have gotten me honour upon Pharaoh, upon his chariots, and upon his horsemen.
19	And the angel of God, which went before the camp of Israel, removed and went behind them; and the pillar of the cloud went from before their face, and stood behind them:
20	And it came between the camp of the Egyptians and the camp of Israel; and it was a cloud and darkness *to them*, but it gave light by night *to these*: so that the one came not near the other all the night.
21	And Moses stretched out his hand over the sea; and the LORD caused the sea to go *back* by a strong east wind all that night, and made the sea dry *land*, and the waters were divided.
22	And the children of Israel went into the midst of the sea upon the dry [ground]: and the waters *were* a wall unto them on their right hand, and on their left.

What does being at the end of a road with seas surrounding you mean? No way forward. No way to run or flee, and the only way to escape takes you into the hands of your enemy. Yet knowing and hearing God will fight for you is something. It is everything, then. But like a dutiful, loving parent, our God does not wish that we should see such a tragedy. As Moses obeys God's commands, God provides a path out of the Red Sea. Many impossible miraculous things take place here. Amongst them is the dry land the Lord God made for the Hebrew people that they may travel sure-footed and not slip and fall.

The pillar that led them, the pillar which was a lamp unto their feet, becomes a pillar of darkness to the Egyptians. This pillar of darkness had to be striking fear in the mighty warriors of Egypt. They had had a taste of darkness already. They could not see the man next to them! Did they feel this darkness as before? We will never know.

God always provides a way. Whether it is a way out of danger or a path to success, God provides. What are you doing to find that path? Are you calling on His name? Are you seeking God's direction? Are you doing what He would desire of you, or are you hiding under a rock living in fear? If our God can do the impossible, shouldn't we believe he can and will protect us?

Dear Lord Jesus,

Help me to see how you clearly direct my feet. Help me to see your Word as that lamp. Lord, help me put away my fears so I may stand boldly for you. That I may go into the unknown and be eager to please you there because you sent me.

In Jesus name, Amen.

DAY #44
EXODUS 14:23-31

23   And the Egyptians pursued, and went in after them to the midst of the sea, *even* all Pharaoh's horses, his chariots, and his horsemen.

24 And it came to pass, that in the morning watch the LORD looked unto the host of the Egyptians through the pillar of fire and of the cloud, and troubled the host of the Egyptians,
25 And took off their chariot wheels, that they drave them heavily: so that the Egyptians said, Let us flee from the face of Israel; for the LORD fighteth for them against the Egyptians.
26 And the LORD said unto Moses, Stretch out your hand over the sea, that the waters may come again upon the Egyptians, upon their chariots, and upon their horsemen.
27 And Moses stretched forth his hand over the sea, and the sea returned to his strength when the morning appeared; and the Egyptians fled against it; and the LORD overthrew the Egyptians in the midst of the sea.
28 And the waters returned, and covered the chariots, and the horsemen, *and* all the host of Pharaoh that came into the sea after them; there remained not so much as one of them.
29 But the children of Israel walked upon dry *land* in the midst of the sea; and the waters *were* a wall unto them on their right hand, and on their left.
30 Thus the LORD saved Israel that day out of the hand of the Egyptians; and Israel saw the Egyptians dead upon the sea shore.
31 And Israel saw that great work which the LORD did upon the Egyptians: and the people feared the LORD, and believed the LORD, and his servant Moses.

"The Lord shall fight for you!" These words should echo in your ears as you read this passage. The Hebrew people seem fickle. But then, most people truly are. They think more about what is confronting them instead of placing their faith in the God who can deliver them. Ask yourself how often God has done something for you while you doubted. So many of us fear and tremble when we are in a horrible situation. We do not stand on the faith He gave us. We need to make the Lord our priority. We must devote part of our lives to him daily in prayer and devotion. Why, because when we really need Him in those horrible times, we will know without a doubt that he can deliver us. We will have sharpened that within us that trusts in the holy and wise God! The more we read His Word, the more we know what God desires. The more we pray, the more we become attuned to having a conversation with the great I AM. But who are we? We, the unworthy sinners, are justified by grace alone. We, the unworthy, are saved by God's grace through the death and resurrection of God's Son. We are joint heirs with Christ, grafted into the vine. He has done so much for us. How can we give so little back? It is time for us believers to get some backbone. We must stand strong for HIM! We must be the light in the darkness!

We must stand on the side of Christ; all other sides matter not. Where does Christ stand? If you do not know anything, you need to spend more time conversing with Him in prayer. Some answers are not yes and no. Some are answers that require your listening ear. Are you ready? Are you ready to be this man or woman for God?

The Hebrew people saw God act and then believed. Do you need a miracle to slap you in the face to grasp what God has done for you? If so, pray. It is possible God will send you one, for our God does impossible things. But do not set up tests for God. Think of all the things He has already shown Himself to you. Look at the morning sunrise and in the sunset.

Dear Lord Jesus,

May you help me to have a strong faith? Help my faith to grow and mature. I want to be that one whose faith stands in You! I want to be the one who gives time, effort, love, and even my tithe to you. Lord, use me. Use me in ways I never imagined to help the lost to find you.

In Jesus name, Amen.

DAY #45
EXODUS 15:1-19

1 Then sang Moses and the children of Israel this song unto the LORD, and had spoken, saying, I will sing unto the LORD, for he hath triumphed gloriously: the horse and his rider hath he thrown into the sea.
2 The LORD *is* my strength and song, and he is become my salvation: he *is* my God, and I will prepare him an habitation; my father's God, and I will exalt him.
3 The LORD *is* a man of war: the LORD *is* his name.
4 Pharaoh's chariots and his host hath he cast into the sea: his chosen captains also are drowned in the Red sea.
5 The depths have covered them: they sank into the bottom as a stone.
6 Your right hand, O LORD, is become glorious in power: your right hand, O LORD, hath dashed in pieces the enemy.
7 And in the greatness of your excellency you have overthrown them that rose up against you: you sent forth your wrath, *which* consumed them as stubble.

8   And with the blast of your nostrils the waters were gathered together, the floods stood upright as an heap, *and* the depths were congealed in the heart of the sea.

9   The enemy said, I will pursue, I will overtake, I will divide the spoil; my lust shall be satisfied upon them; I will draw my sword, my hand shall destroy them.

10 You did blow with your wind, the sea covered them: they sank as lead in the mighty waters.

11 Who *is* like unto you, O LORD, among the gods? who *is* like you, glorious in holiness, fearful *in* praises, doing wonders?

12 You stretched out your right hand, the earth swallowed them.

13 You in your mercy have led forth the people *which* you have redeemed: you have guided *them* in your strength unto your holy habitation.

14 The people shall hear, *and* be afraid: sorrow shall take hold on the inhabitants of Palestina.

15 Then the dukes of Edom shall be amazed; the mighty men of Moab, trembling shall take hold upon them; all the inhabitants of Canaan shall melt away.

16 Fear and dread shall fall upon them; by the greatness of your arm they shall be *as* still as a stone; till your people pass over, O LORD, till the people pass over, *which* you hast purchased.

17 You shalt bring them in, and plant them in the mountain of your inheritance, *in* the place, O LORD, *which* you have made for you to dwell in, *in* the Sanctuary, O Lord, *which* your hands have established.

18 The LORD shall reign for ever and ever.

19 For the horse of Pharaoh went in with his chariots and with his horsemen into the sea, and the LORD brought again the waters of the sea upon them; but the children of Israel went on dry *land* in the midst of the sea.

The day the Egyptians died pursuing them into the Red Sea was the first day the Hebrew people truly felt free from bondage. They had walked for about three days before reaching the end of Egypt's wilderness—the point of the Sinai Peninsula. They walked and ran after God opened the Red Sea to get to the other side. Probably not without much awe and wonder at how this was even possible. Even their song of praise recognizes the miracle of having crossed on dry land. But it was that moment when God had the sea swallow up the Egyptians that a cry of victory arose in the tongues of Hebrew slaves as they now understood their God had freed them.

Can you imagine your family walking free for the first time in generations, with no one ordering you to do this or that? No one threatens you if you do not obey them. No one posing as a threat to your freedom or harm to your children had to be a big weight lifted. When fear weighs on you, it shackles you so much that chains are not needed. This song came about as an expression of joy that those shackles were finally gone. They were free – free to be who they were and to serve the God who chose them.

Dear Lord Jesus,

How the mighty fall when You are present. You stand alone in Your awesome power. You alone have the power to save. You are the only worthy God deserving of worship. Lord, use me as part of Your plan to share the glories of your awesome and powerful love with others.

In Jesus name, Amen.

DAY #46
EXODUS 15:20-27

20 And Miriam the prophetess, the sister of Aaron, took a timbrel in her hand; and all the women went out after her with timbrels and with dances.
21 And Miriam answered them, Sing you to the LORD, for he hath triumphed gloriously; the horse and his rider hath he thrown into the sea.
22 So Moses brought Israel from the Red sea, and they went out into the wilderness of Shur; and they went three days in the wilderness, and found no water.
23 And when they came to Marah, they could not drink of the waters of Marah, for they *were* bitter: therefore the name of it was called Marah.
24 And the people murmured against Moses, saying, What shall we drink?
25 And he cried unto the LORD; and the LORD showed him a tree, *which* when he had cast into the waters, the waters were made sweet: there he made for them a statute and an ordinance, and there he proved them,
26 And said, If you wilt diligently hearken to the voice of the LORD your God, and wilt do that which is right in his sight, and will give ear to his commandments, and keep all his statutes, I will put none of these diseases upon you, which I have brought upon the Egyptians: for I *am* the LORD that heals you.

27 And they came to Elim, where *were* twelve wells of water, and threescore and ten palm trees: and they encamped there by the waters.

It seems that the people do not see God as personal. They see him as a distant, unreachable God who is fickle about his concern for them. They do not yet have faith. They praise God after miracles and shortly after that, forget His provision. How that is possible pretty much boggles the mind. They would not be where they are without Him. They would still be in bondage serving their Egyptian masters. Not one of them does not know this. This makes one think that many have yet to pray to God in their journey. They see Moses as the person who speaks to God for them, so they do not even think of it.

As a child, I went to a church where the Pastor shared two sermons every week. One for the children and one for the adults. The children's moments were brief and made sense; they impacted my life. As a teen listening to the same pastor, this continued. But the thought of reading the Bible as part of my daily need to serve God was missing. I thought that was what the pastor did for me. I had been taught at home to pray before meals and when I went to bed. These moments were ingrained within me. But I still had no grasp of the need to know more about God or His love for me.

What can we do to change this? How can we make others see that God is personal and is there for them? How can we make others see that the God of the Bible desires that everyone should read His Word and pray to Him on a regular basis? What are you doing that could change this? Setting that example is the best way. Share your devotions with others. Let people see this as part of your life. Let them see how it impacts you. Show them that we serve a personal God, and we have to be personal with Him. That means reading His word and communicating with Him in prayer.

Dear Lord Jesus,

Use us, Lord, that we may help others see that You alone are the great God of love who desires so much for us. Find ways for us to share our devotions on a daily basis. Give us that push to share Your Word and then a push to pray with others whenever the chance arises. Use us, Lord. Help us that we may change the world into one that thinks of You first.

In Jesus name, Amen.

DAY #47
EXODUS 16:1-3

1   And they took their journey from Elim, and all the congregation of the children of Israel came unto the wilderness of Sin, which *is* between Elim and Sinai, on the fifteenth day of the second month after their departing out of the land of Egypt.

2   And the whole congregation of the children of Israel murmured against Moses and Aaron in the wilderness:

3   And the children of Israel said unto them, Would to God we had died by the hand of the LORD in the land of Egypt, when we sat by the flesh pots, *and* when we did eat bread to

the full; for you have brought us forth into this wilderness, to kill this whole assembly with hunger.

There are many questions posed in these three verses. Were Moses and Aaron's families any different in their needs? Had they some alternative food source? Had they prepared better? Was their need the same, and did they not complain because they believed God would provide?

Their need likely were the same, and the faith of Moses and Aaron understood the power of God and feared petitioning God for their personal need vs. the needs of the Hebrew people.

So what do we know? The word wilderness here does not mean what it means today. To them, it meant a land without food sources. No vegetation. Very few animals. When traveling, the Hebrew people walked about 5 and a half hours a day. Think of how many were there with Moses. In 12:37, it states that there were 600,000 men. Only the men here were counted, not women and not children. So, the number could be larger than 2,000,000. How do you feed so many mouths? God had a plan. Sometimes even our grumbles over our needs and wants are used by God. This is one of those times.

Are your needs put before God? Do you seek him out as the answer to your needs? Think about this.

Dear Lord Jesus,

You know my wants and needs before I know them. You are my great provider. Lord, never let me forget that. Help me to never forget your wants are more important than anything I need. What you desire for my life is more important than anything. For you have given me a key to heaven through Your shed blood on the cross.

In Jesus name, Amen.

DAY #48
EXODUS 16:4-21

4   Then said the LORD unto Moses, Behold, I will rain bread from heaven for you; and the people shall go out and gather a certain rate every day, that I may prove them, whether they will walk in my law, or no.
5   And it shall come to pass, that on the sixth day they shall prepare *that* which they bring in; and it shall be twice as much as they gather daily.
6   And Moses and Aaron said unto all the children of Israel, At even, then ye shall know that the LORD hath brought you out from the land of Egypt:
7   And in the morning, then ye shall see the glory of the LORD; for that he heareth your murmurings against the LORD: and what *are* we, that you murmur against us?
8   And Moses said, *This shall be*, when the LORD shall give you in the evening flesh to eat, and in the morning bread to the full; for that the LORD hears your murmurings which yeou murmur against him: and what *are* we? your murmurings *are* not against us, but against the LORD.
9   And Moses spake unto Aaron, Say unto all the congregation of the children of Israel, Come near before the LORD: for he hath heard your murmurings.

10   And it came to pass, as Aaron spake unto the whole congregation of the children of Israel, that they looked toward the wilderness, and, behold, the glory of the LORD appeared in the cloud.

11   And the LORD spake unto Moses, saying,

12   I have heard the murmurings of the children of Israel: speak unto them, saying, At even you shall eat flesh, and in the morning you shall be filled with bread; and you shall know that I *am* the LORD your God.

13   And it came to pass, that at even the quails came up, and covered the camp: and in the morning the dew lay round about the host.

14   And when the dew that lay was gone up, behold, upon the face of the wilderness *there lay* a small round thing, *as* small as the hoar frost on the ground.

15   And when the children of Israel saw *it*, they said one to another, It *is* manna: for they did not know what it *was*. And Moses said unto them, This *is* the bread which the LORD hath given you to eat.

16   This *is* the thing which the LORD hath commanded, Gather of it every man according to his eating, an omer for every man, *according to* the number of your persons; take you every man for *them* which *are* in his tents.

17   And the children of Israel did so, and gathered, some more, some less.

18   And when they did mete *it* with an omer, he that gathered much had nothing over, and he that gathered little had no lack; they gathered every man according to his eating.

19   And Moses said, Let no man leave of it till the morning.

20   Notwithstanding they hearkened not unto Moses; but some of them left of it until the morning, and it bred worms, and stank: and Moses was wroth with them.

21   And they gathered it every morning, every man according to his eating: and when the sun waxed hot, it melted.

It's almost as if the Hebrew people needed lessons to understand that the God who delivered them from bondage in Egypt was a personal God. He heard their pleas and delivered them. Now He hears their murmurings against his chosen spokesman and again answers them. God recognizes that this need for food was of His making since He brought 600,000 men out of Egypt, not counting the women and children. This does not even take into account whatever livestock they brought with them.

Manna from heaven and birds that come simply to allow you to kill them for food. Can you imagine the strangeness of this that no one needed a weapon to shoot them? They arrived for God's purpose – to become dinner for the Hebrew people. What would you think if you lived on that side of the Red Sea and saw this vast amount of people arrive out of the Red Sea and walk into a land devoid of food to feed them? What would you think if you saw them living and breathing blissfully because this God of their daily provision provided for them?

This incredible provision came with limitations that so many are willing to press for some reason. Like babies test to see what their boundaries are. Some refused to be obedient, took more than they needed, and did not get rid of what was left over. They thought they could have a day of rest if they gathered extra. God did not desire that people could take any day off that they wanted. He had a planned day of rest for them – the seventh day.

Dear Lord Jesus,

Thank you for planning to meet my needs before I know them. Thank you for providing for me in more ways than I can even grasp. You are the great and almighty God. You are the one, and only whom salvation comes from. Lord, allow me to honor you by sharing who you are with the world. Lord, may I be part of Your plan to share your great love with the world.

In Jesus name, Amen.

DAY #49
EXODUS 16:22-31

22 And it came to pass, *that* on the sixth day they gathered twice as much bread, two omers for one *man*: and all the rulers of the congregation came and told Moses.
23 And he said unto them, This *is that* which the LORD hath said, Tomorrow *is* the rest of the holy sabbath unto the LORD: bake *that* which you will bake *today*, and seethe that you will seethe; and that which remains over lay up for you to be kept until the morning.
24 And they laid it up till the morning, as Moses bade: and it did not stink, neither was there any worm therein.
25 And Moses said, Eat that today; for today *is* a sabbath unto the LORD: today you shall not find it in the field.
26 Six days you shall gather it; but on the seventh day, *which is* the sabbath, in it there shall be none.
27 And it came to pass, *that* there went out *some* of the people on the seventh day for to gather, and they found none.

28   And the LORD said unto Moses, How long refuse you to keep my commandments and my laws?
29   See, for that the LORD hath given you the sabbath, therefore he giveth you on the sixth day the bread of two days; abide you every man in his place, let no man go out of his place on the seventh day.
30   So the people rested on the seventh day.
31   And the house of Israel called the name thereof Manna: and it *was* like coriander seed, white; and the taste of it *was* like wafers *made* with honey.

God has a deeper interest in us than we know. He used our need for food to teach us about the Sabbath – the seventh day is a day of rest. It's almost as if people are so stubborn that change is not something they easily take. I admit that is true for me at times. But after seeing miracle after miracle, you would think they would easily accept what they were told. As I thought about this, I began to think about how sometimes we fight against change. We do things to be stubborn and go against the grain. Even regarding our daily time with Christ doing devotions, how often do things try to prevent us from enjoying our time with the Creator? How many times do we give in and put God second? This is no different than what we see the Hebrew people doing here. God is training them to love the Sabbath.

God's deeper interest in us is also shown in the flavoring. This taste of God's bread from heaven is sweet. It has flavor! It awakens a sense of excitement in your tastebuds. God designed us. He knows that this is something the Hebrew people would love. He designed our tastebuds. He understands what awakens them, and He knows what they desire.

Dear Lord Jesus,

May YOU, oh Lord, be magnified in your goodness to us. Your provision comes with blessings we do not even grasp. Even as you placed manna before the Hebrew people every waking day, you made it with the thought of how good it would taste to them. You care more for us than we can comprehend. Lord, help me to see your provision as beyond comprehension. For you know my needs before I even know I have a need. You plan for my provision long before my need arises. God, you truly are to be glorified.

In Jesus name, Amen.

DAY #50
EXODUS 16:32-36

32 And Moses said, This *is* the thing which the LORD commands, Fill an omer of it to be kept for your generations; that they may see the bread wherewith I have fed you in the wilderness, when I brought you forth from the land of Egypt.
33 And Moses said unto Aaron, Take a pot, and put an omer full of manna therein, and lay it up before the LORD, to be kept for your generations.
34 As the LORD commanded Moses, so Aaron laid it up before the Testimony, to be kept.

35 And the children of Israel did eat manna forty years, until they came to a land inhabited; they did eat manna, until they came unto the borders of the land of Canaan.

36 Now an omer *is* the tenth *part* of an ephah.

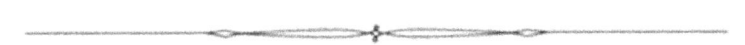

An "omer," according to BibleStudyTools.com is equal in volume to a half gallon. This makes sense, considering how much a person would need to eat to feel satisfied. An omer is also how much was set aside as God commanded to be kept for generations. When you think about this, it makes you wonder. Doesn't all the manna turn to worms when it's kept too long? But God can preserve that which he desires. Perhaps for others, seeing that God could preserve this when others had an expiration date would be a source of hope. Hebrews 9:4 tells us that it would later be placed in the Ark of Covenant.

This is a hint that God can and will preserve His Word.

Dear Lord Jesus,

You are the great and living God. You are able to do more than I can imagine. Your love for us is shown in the preservation of Your Word and in Your death on the cross for our sins. We serve none of Your mercy. Yet Your love makes molds and makes us so much better than the person we thought we were. Lord, continue to work on me. Make me into that person who easily shares Your love with others. Lord, put me in that spot to share who You are with those who do not know You.

In Jesus name, Amen.

www.ingramcontent.com/pod-product-compliance
Lightning Source LLC
LaVergne TN
LVHW020442070526
838199LV00063B/4829